Ullans 15

Ullans

THE MAGAZINE FOR ULSTER-SCOTS

Nummer 15, Ware 2018

Edited by Anne Smyth

ULLANS PRESS

COLLOGUE O ULLANS

Compluthert fur tae gie a heft til tha Ulstèr-Scotch Leid in wor ain hamely tongue an litèrarie scrievins fae tha Lallans o Ulstèr.

ULLANS is published by the Ulster-Scots Language Society

The Ulster-Scots Language Society was formed to encourage an interest in traditional Ulster-Scots literature; to promote creative writing in modern Ulster-Scots; to support the use of Ulster-Scots speech and writing in present-day education; and to encourage the Ulster-Scots tradition in music, dance, song, ballads and story-telling. In short, our aim is to promote the status of Ulster-Scots as a traditional language, and to re-establish its dignity as a European regional language with an important part to play in our cultural heritage.

ISBN 978-1-905281-33-6

Cover image of Stonechat courtesy of Charles J Sharp
www.sharpphotography.co.uk

Contents

Editorial

As the content of this issue of *Ullans* is being prepared, the question of language is at the centre of controversy on conditions required for the re-establishment of the Stormont institutions, "collapsed" by Sinn Fein on the ground of government mismanagement of the Renewable Heat Initiative. However, it seems that Sinn Fein co-operation in efforts to reactivate the Legislative Assembly is not conditional upon anything to do with grants for boilers, but instead depends primarily upon the enshrining in law of a privileged position for the Irish language.

No doubt there is much to support the view that political factors are prominent in the thinking behind the campaign for an Irish language act, not least the obvious lack of facility with the language on the part of most of the political leaders who advocate it. Our own experience leads us fully to sympathise with any genuine Irish language enthusiasts watching their language reduced to being used as a political bargaining chip (although there has been little documentary evidence of public statements to this effect).

As matters stand, the largest unionist party seems to be determined not to concede an Irish language act, and stalemate has ensued. In the course of the negotiations there were indications that participants were considering incorporating some provision for Ulster-Scots in legal protection measures. Consequently, on the 29th of May 2017, the USLS wrote to the First Minister to put its point of view on these suggestions. We appealed to her not to consider putting in place "balancing" legislation for Ulster-Scots unless there is a radical change of direction from what has previously applied. The tinkering of civil servants in matters of Ulster-Scots language development when they have neither the skills nor the commitment to direct them has done little to help and much to hinder.

The Language Society has always taken a resolutely apolitical stance, which places it in a different category from most Irish language activists, many of whose statements have been unhelpful. Implications of an ulterior motive arising from the use of such phrases as "nation building" are to be expected. However, the irony in the application of other terms like "equality" and "respect" has not been lost on Ulster-Scots activists.

Recently, the *Belfast News Letter* reported that £190 million had been spent on Irish between 2010 and 2017. Figures for the period between the Belfast Agreement and 2010 appear harder to obtain. Contributing to the huge disparity in the financial provision for Irish as opposed to Ulster-Scots, we have the existence of at least a dozen Irish language organisations which obtain funding, in comparison with the total lack of funding for the USLS, now apparently the only body that prioritises the Ulster-Scots language rather than an undefined "culture".

The Belfast Agreement itself institutionalised the disparity by creating an Ulster-Scots "Boord" that is half the size of its Irish counterpart and contains vastly fewer members who self-identify as speakers of the respective language. Possibly most telling of all is the generally unacknowledged fact that the component parts of Foras na Gaeilge pre-existed the Belfast Agreement by many decades and were simply slotted into the mechanisms created by the agreement. This would seem to imply that they achieved little during those intervening decades despite the large sums injected by the southern government into expanding knowledge of the language beyond the Gaeltacht regions. In an anonymous blog dated 29 July 2013, the writer began with the following paragraph:

> The authoritative form of a language is that spoken by its native speakers. In most countries, this is not a controversial proposition, because in most countries the official language is widely spoken. In Ireland, the pretence remains that Irish is the official language. I say it is a pretence, as nearly all work in government departments is done through English, and in most cases it is done by people who couldn't do it in any other language. The official working language is English.

This text, perhaps unsurprisingly, has been removed from the internet, but a copy is available from the USLS on request.

In Northern Ireland, the Irish language is supported by capital expenditure on a breath-taking scale. Within the walled city of Londonderry is now situated "Cultúrlann Uí Chanáin", which according to its website is "a purpose-built Irish language, cultural and enterprise centre". The building accommodates a 200 seat theatre, a multi-purpose arts centre and a conference centre, costing £4 million to construct.

Further examination would no doubt produce more examples, but even this cursory glance at expenditure on Irish seems to show that the inequality its supporters claim is being experienced by the language is a very strange kind of inequality. On the capital expenditure issue alone, Ulster-Scots activists were meanwhile being told that their demand for a fully-resourced physical Ulster-Scots Academy, promised by the Direct Rule government as far back as June 2005, was unrealistic and they would have to settle for a "virtual Academy". In relation to the language, that too remains undelivered, but it would in any case be superfluous, given the existence of our own website, www.ulsterscotsacademy.com, created, augmented and maintained at our own expense.

The final term bandied about is "respect", usually allied to criticism of Gregory Campbell's "curry my yoghurt" statement in the Assembly back in November 2014. Martin McGuinness said this "bordered on racist" (yet the Society in complaining about the scurrilous Knox cartoons in the *Irish News* found that Ulster-Scots do not qualify as a disparate racial group and therefore have no protection). The headline of Liam Clarke's article on the subject of Gregory Campbell's intervention, in the *Belfast Telegraph*, labelled it "pidgin Irish". Time without number, Ulster-Scots language speakers have been confronted with state-sponsored pastiches of Ulster-Scots and been expected to take no offence. In this instance too, the "respect" seems to operate only in one direction. And let us not even refer to the sudden absence of Ulster-Scots titles of Stormont departments from their branding – Stormont no longer functions, after all.

Ulster-Scots would not presume to criticise any Irish language translations, because we are fully aware that we do not know enough about the subject – but everyone is an expert when it comes to Ulster-Scots. This can obscure the fact that there are language development dilemmas common to both – dilemmas which the uninformed selectively employ as a stick with which to beat Ulster-Scots. Unfortunately, it does not seem possible that the two regional minority languages might make common cause to safeguard minority language rights.

The blog of 29 July 2013 quoted above is a well written, closely reasoned critique of the work of Coiste Téarmaíochta, which is the part of Foras na Gaeilge that deals with devising Irish terminology for modern referents. It explains the problem as follows:

> … (F)or political reasons, the official language is stated as being Irish, and everything must be translated into Irish. The problem is that Irish is a language only spoken natively in small farming or fishing communities. If Irish had remained the language of all, then scientists, politicians, academics, journalists and others would all have had Irish as their first language, and the vocabulary needed for every sphere of life would have evolved naturally. But as this is not the case, vocabulary is being invented by a *Coiste Téarmaíochta* to fill the gaps.

Does this sound familiar? But of course Ulster-Scots has no body equivalent to Coiste Téarmaíochta, and more importantly no accreditation scheme for translators.

There follows a detailed critique of some of the terms coined by Coiste, adducing the Galway Gaeltacht native speaker Conor Keane's condemnation of what he calls "Gobbledegaeilge" and the criticisms of Feargal Ó Béarra, another native speaker and an academic at NUI Galway, of specific incorrect vocabulary. The writer points out that technical terms such as "cathode-ray oscilloscope" were devised by native speakers of English to begin with and are in daily use by native speakers of English *who work in the professional sphere where the terms are relevant.* That, of course, leads to a major difficulty in that the blogger is advocating viewing the neologisms as wrong *unless and until* they are adopted in native speech – but of course there isn't much call for this kind of vocabulary in rural and fishing communities.

In the course of his argument, the writer states:

> There is a difficulty here, as most native speakers of Irish, as Feargal Ó Béarra pointed out in his article, do not read Irish. The Irish

language – at the *native* end of the Irish-using community, at least – has become more or less a purely spoken language. While not totally so, as there are Gaeltacht novelists, it is largely so. There is a mismatch, therefore, between the *spoken language of the Gaeltacht* and the written, official language found in the artifical [sic] so-called Standard. Where native speakers hardly ever read or write a language, the language quickly loses an official register of speech, a register that the Coiste Téarmaíochta is clearly trying to summon into existence for the purposes of official translation.

He or she adds: "If native speakers in the Gaeltacht don't read Irish, then new words cannot spread too far".

This blogger's knowledge is clearly of Munster Irish, which appears to be predominant even in Ulster among those who have acquired the language by what we would call *buik lear*, as opposed to intergenerational transfer (which is the way in which Ulster-Scots is almost always learnt). However, the analysis is painstaking and salutary; and, so far as the conclusion can be encapsulated in a sentence, he or she appears to be saying that Coiste Téarmaíochta has cut itself off from contact with native speakers of Irish, creates its own terminology uninformed by native vocabulary, and is prioritising protecting the vested interests of a cadre of professional "translators" that are similarly estranged from the real language. He or she says: "In another context, these translators might wax lyrical over the role of British rule in eroding the Irish language, while overlooking their own contempt for native Irish and the role of their made-up Standard in weakening the language in the Gaeltacht".

Stripped of the specifics, this piece could almost have been written about Ulster-Scots; however, the common dilemmas and difficulties may well be a natural outcome of the assumption of state control over language. Language development is the business of native speakers and the organisations that represent them – not the state. And the Ulster-Scots Language Society is proud of its record of prioritising the needs of native speakers while resisting the tendency of state institutions to consider themselves, despite the absence of any background in the language, to be the sole repositories of all knowledge, skills and discernment on related matters.

Given the confusion caused by the suspension of Stormont, readers will not be surprised to know that the scheduled review by the Committee of Experts from Strasbourg on the operation of the European Charter for Regional or Minority Languages, due in July 2017, does not appear to have taken place. It is likely that the cause of this was the lack of a report from the Department for Communities on support for Ulster-Scots and Irish. The absence of a review cannot be expected to be detrimental to Ulster-Scots, as our language never seems to have received any benefit from the government's ratification of the Charter anyway. On the last occasion, the Society could not meet the representatives of the Committee of Experts because we were not informed they were intending to visit Northern Ireland. In response to our protest, we were invited to submit a position paper, which we duly did, only to find that it had been completely ignored. Previous CoE reports made much of the erroneous impression given to those taking part in the review that any action taken to support Ulster-Scots would obstruct provision for Irish, and nothing said by the Society to challenge this false assumption was countenanced. The last available report read:

> "adopt a strategy to enhance and develop Ulster Scots, in co-operation with the speakers".

> 19. The position of Ulster Scots has improved since the previous monitoring round, thanks largely to the work of Tha Boord o Ulstèr-Scotch (Ulster-Scots Agency), which has had a proactive role in developing a strategy for Ulster Scots, based on firm language planning grounds.

The Society remains confused about what these "language planning grounds" might be; nor have we seen much sign of "cooperation with the speakers". Previous experience of the obscure workings of the Charter, however, means that we do not expect it to be of any great assistance in the promotion and protection of Ulster-Scots.

Apart from inevitable involvement in the issues discussed above, the Society has also been active in producing good quality Ulster-Scots publications. In September 2017 an event was held as part of the Ballywalter Festival, to launch three new books published by The Ullans Press, publishing arm of the USLS. These were: Jim Fenton, *On Slaimish*; Philip Robinson, *Oul Licht, New Licht and other Ulster-Scots Poems*; and May de la Cherois Crommelin, *Orange Lily*. This last book was originally published in 1879 and is set in Carrowdore. The Society is grateful to those who sponsored this last publication, which has proved very popular with members and friends.

On 12th November 2016, a launch took place of the *Tha Fower Gospels: Matthew, Mark, Luke and John in Ulster-Scots* in Greyabbey Presbyterian Church. It was a most uplifting event, enjoyed by everyone who was there, and it was great to see the work of the translation teams over so many months come to such satisfactory fruition. We'd like again to record our thanks to all those who helped in any way with the launches (you know who you are!), including all our courageous readers, the Low Country Boys, and Jim Shannon MP, who did sterling service as "launcher" at both events.

A spin-off from the Academy website on social media has produced some very interesting vocabulary items and photographs, and continues to be a lively forum for an increasing band of Ulster-Scots aficionados.

The "old hands" among our members will realise that the Society has reached the 25th anniversary milestone. It is nothing short of a miracle that it has so long survived all the vicissitudes and hostilities of life in the world of Ulster-Scots. Having lived through it all once, we are not inclined to give a reprise of "the blood, sweat and tears"; but it would be remiss of us not to thank all those who have identified with the Society in its struggles during that quarter century, often at great personal cost, and those who have contributed their writings to this journal for the enjoyment and encouragement of us all.

It would be wrong to finish this editorial without reference to the new writers who feature in this issue of *Ullans*. In an article for *Études Irlandaises* in early 2013, we noted: "over the years *Ullans* has featured approximately 75 different modern writers in or about Ulster-Scots (including around 10 from outside Northern Ireland), and the work of 19 different historic writers". The total of these writers from previous issues of *Ullans* at that time was something of a surprise; however, it was impossible not to be encouraged by the discovery, and it helps to justify our claim that *Ullans* is the only publication in Northern Ireland that is dedicated primarily to showcasing new Ulster-Scots writers. We extend a hearty welcome to all the new writers whose work forms part of *Ullans 15*, and we hope that you will continue to develop your skills and submit material for future issues.

Nesca Robb of Lisnabreeny, 1905-1976

Billy McCullough

It was on a spring day, in May of 2014, that a sizeable and knowledgeable crowd gathered in the small village of Moneyreagh. The occasion was twofold: to witness the unveiling of a Blue Plaque to Robert Huddleston, more often referred to as 'The Bard of Moneyreagh' and, secondly, to witness the opening of a Memorial Park dedicated to five Ulster-Scots writers, all poets except for the novelist Charlotte Cowan. These five were: Francis Boyle, Charlotte Cowan, Robert Brown, Nesca Robb and Robert Huddleston. Each of the poets had in their own way committed to verse a lasting yet forgotten legacy, using the Ulster-Scots tongue to promote a wider understanding and appreciation of their culture and rural traditions. Nesca Robb was identified as one of those intriguing individuals and therefore proven worthy of having aspects of her life brought back into focus.

Miss Robb was born in Ireland just a few years into the twentieth century, on the 27th of May 1905, and described herself proudly as a child of Belfast. Nesca was born at 'Ballyhackmore House', Dundela, the second daughter of Charles and Agnes Robb. Her older sibling Grace had been born on the 28th of June 1898. Ballyhackamore House, which Nesca describes in depth and with great affection, was where she spent many of her adolescent years; but regrettably this has been demolished. During 1920, her parents moved to a property at Groomsport known as 'The Banks', a move which instead of bringing pleasure brought misfortune and family bereavement.

Nesca Adeline Robb

Margaret Wilson   Oct. 27, 1923
(A Scottish Covenanter executed 1685)

'Gie me yir hand, ma Margaret,
Fa the are few an the [...]
An' leave the [...] o' the Kirks an crouds
An' come my bride to be.'

'An' it's oh, an't be ye cruel o' mine
I will ne'er lo'e the mair
But I'm gonna forsake the faith that's mine
Or break the with I sweare.'

'Oh speak nae mair, my ain Margaret —
Yir [laws] are ill an' strong
An' thought I stood afel my guid heart's blood
Yir [witness] sweer ye lang.'

'There's a fell slate by Solway
An' could, an' saltle's the sea
An' gin ye keep your covenant
[Freilor]'s in death ye'll dee.'

they've the [underclown] to Solway
Till whar the tide was low
An' [Jeanie] lies in her guid heart's blood
That was [bell] to [lift] the [...]

An' syne came in the salt-salt sea
An' syne came in the foam
An' aye whaur came one [harper]
She [named] sair guid lost's warm.

Oh slow an' could the waves water
[Pare] yir aboon his knee
An' so oft lieleog or till an' fell
She leas blunded her [sic]

'[heir] fare ye well, my ain [mither]
It's nain, nain will ye greit
When they sad bring my [chonner] corse [haime]
An' lay it at your feet'

'An' fare ye well, my ain faither'

102

103

From Nesca Robb's notebook — a poem dedicated to the Scottish Covenanter Margaret Wilson

Her grandfather was John Robb of the department store that bore his name, established in Belfast during 1857. By the age of ten, having been tutored privately at home by her governess, she was enrolled at Richmond Lodge School, Malone, in 1915. In her memoirs she describes this school as "small, friendly, un-competitive, rather a freak school". Her education completed, Miss Robb moved to Somerville, Oxford, where she studied Modern Languages and Philosophy, meeting individuals who broadened her mind. C S Lewis had been, you might say, a close neighbour, since he too lived in the Dundela vicinity. Although Lewis was her senior by a few years, both attended Oxford University during overlapping years, so there is every possibility, indeed likelihood, that their paths may have crossed.

Having considered the pedigree of Miss Robb, you might still be wondering about her accreditation and suitability for inclusion in *Ullans* magazine. Her personal memoirs comprise a collection of poems in four volumes, simply presented but obviously penned in her own handwriting. Further reading suggests that in 1919, at the tender age of fourteen, she was committing thoughts to verse, perhaps simply, yet logically, with clarity and in rhyme. It has been proposed that the Ulster poet Richard Rowley may have been an influential figure during her developing career; doubtless there must have been others. It is also obvious that she was familiar with, and aware of, the Ulster-Scots tongue and undoubtedly had heard it spoken in certain locations associated with North Down.

At an early age, the senior members of the Robb family (uncles and aunts who lived at Lisnabreeny) instilled in her the background knowledge relating to her family roots. Nesca commits to paper the understanding that her Protestant ancestors came to Ulster from Scotland, possibly as early as 1620. Allegedly, some became involved with the United Irishmen, receiving harsh treatment when identified and arrested. Nesca was extremely proud of these family disclosures relating to historical events, and on more than one occasion used such events to great effect. The following opening verse must have been produced at an early age, although it is undated and perhaps some might regard it as simplistic.

Betsy Gray – a ballad of '98

Goodbye, goodbye, my father dear
For I must go away
To fight for the sake of this dear, dear land
When the men go forth to-day.

During October of 1923, around the time she went up to Oxford, Nesca wrote this opening verse to a poem dedicated to the Scottish Covenanter Margaret Wilson, using Ulster-Scots to great effect.

Gie me aye kiss faer Margaret,
For the love I bear tae thee
A'n leave the clash o' the kirks and creeds
A'n come my bride tae be.

Her first collection, *Poems*, was published in 1939. It contains over 30 short poems on the natural landscape, largely inspired by the countryside around Lisnabreeny House. In fact, there are four poems with 'Lisnabreeny' in the title: 'Lisnabreeny: The Snowdrops'; 'Lisnabreeny: Early Spring'; 'Lisnabreeny: Evening'; and 'Lisnabreeny: September'. In 'The Watcher', the setting of Lisnabreeny is unnamed, but unquestionably intended. This poem is, in its last verse, almost a dedication of Lisnabreeny to those National Trust visitors that would be able to enjoy the same sights. (She donated Lisnabreeny to the National Trust only two years before this poem was published).

The Watcher

Where bracken rusts along the hill
Our summer walks are overgrown
The air, like standing water chill
Spreads moisture over tree and stone.

And down the opening valley grey,
Where crawls the lead-cold Lagan stream,
The limber sallies scarcely sway
Against the evening's baleful gleam,

That through the silence promises
A night of storm, whose voice shall be
For you a heralding of bliss;
The severing of my life to me.

It also features two pieces that show her awareness of Ulster-Scots
vocabulary and speech which she must have heard during her
childhood in Belfast and Castlereagh:

Hallow E'en

Who are ye ridin', ridin', ridin'
Ridin' down on the wind to-night
I'm hunkered down by a thorn bush hidin'
An' nary a star gies light.

Loose on the wind wi' their hoof-beats ringin'
Wild black horses race through the air,
An' on them the ghaists ride schreichin' an' singin'
Fleein' tae God knows where*

A curlew skirls ower the bogland heather
Far off there's a roar frae the drumlie sea

The black trees twist in the cauld black weather
An' the cauld rain soaks through me.

Och, who are ye ridin', ridin', ridin',
Singin' thunderin', over me head?
Will ye find me still wherever I'm hidin'
Oh ye ghaists o' the dead?

* This may be a reference to *The Man from God Knows Where*,
United Irishman Thomas Russell, who was hidden in Cregagh
Glen by James Witherspoon of Knockbracken.

Blind

Oh bonny thrush, ye wee brown bird
You've got the heart of song
It's lang, sae lang, since I seen the light
Though it's warm on me face an' strong.

Tell me birdie, you that hev eyes,
Are the whins on fire again?
Do the buds come after the winter yet
An' the rainbow after the rain?

Oh bonny thrush, ye wee brown bird
Ye've the bloom on the blackthorn tree
An' the blue sky's lift, and the changein' days
But they're over and done for me.

Her autobiography, *An Ulsterwoman in England 1924-1941*, recounts her experiences of moving to England and of the cultural
differences she found, which initially caused her great discomfort.

'... The Ulsterman's reticence does not spoil either his appetite for a '*crack*'*, or his essential friendliness.' [p. 2 footnote: *'*A crack*' = gossip, chat]

'Anyone who lived in a place so ludicrously named as Wimbledon need not think a word like Ballyhackamore peculiar. They might pour scorn on me for some odd pronunciation ... but they were poor ignoramuses who had never tasted potato bread and didn't know what you meant by '*deuking*' or '*speiling*'* ...'. [p. 6 footnote: *To '*deuk*' is to dodge about, to '*spiel*' is to climb, especially up a 'spieling rope'.]

She understood Ulster as a 'three stranded' cultural blend:

'... the Ulster dialects, with their basis of Lowland Scots, their borrowings from the Gaelic, their echoes of Elizabethan English and their individual colour as of the fields that nurtured them, are an image of the mixed psychological factors, here in fusion, there in conflict, that make the Ulsterman by no means the simple block of stone that his enemies like to depict ...'

The cultural differences she felt on moving to England involved political identity as well as linguistic:

'I was born a little Unionist, bred royalist and loyalist from the start. My early memories are loud with the excitement of days when even the mildest of one's acquaintances was indulging in gun-running and unlawful assembly' (p. 9).

'In common with most of our fellow citizens, we watched the fare-well parade of our own Ulster Division. On that occasion, having cheered myself hoarse, I hung so far out the window [presumably at her father's premises in Castle Place, where the parade passed] to acclaim Lord Carson that I all but precipitated myself head first at my hero's feet. Not so many months later, that Division, fighting valiantly, was cut to pieces at the Somme' (p. 29).

Her 1939 book of poems illustrates the full range of her versatility. She published a final collection of poetry, *Ards Ecologues*, in 1970, defining at the outset of the publication an 'ecologue' as a 'short poem on a rural subject'. These 'ecologues' reveal that her literary skill extended beyond describing the natural landscape of north Down and the Castlereagh hills in *Poems* (1939), into a beautiful and sensitive recording of the speech, customs and character of local folklife.

In *Ards Ecologues* there is a short poem on Cregagh Glen called 'The Glen in Winter', but it also includes interesting longer poems called 'The Storm' (a personal favourite), 'The Primrose', 'July', and 'The Harvest', which are full of classic descriptions of rural Ulster life – a tartan rug, a scripture verse on the wall, a Bible and a copy of the *Life of Henry Cooke*, fresh soda bread and a portrait of William of Orange. Here we meet such characters as the 'foundered postman, Geordie Black' and old 'Annie Millar', using words like *farl, happed up, outbye, wag-at-wall, sprauchle, crack, cloddin, forbye, thrawn, miched, loanin* and many other Ulster-Scots words and phrases.

Miss Robb spent a large portion of her busy life abroad before returning home and, as an act of benevolence, donating her grandfather's property, 'Lisnabreeny House' to the National Trust for the enjoyment of the public. Miss Robb never married, dedicating her life to poetry, literature, the arts and historical writings. Her publications include, *Four in Exile* (1945), *An Ulsterwoman in England* (1942), the two volume *History of William of Orange*, and of course those two books of poetry.

Dr Nesca Robb was a scholar and intellectual, yet remained approachable and knowledgeable on numerous subjects. She died in England and her ashes were interred with her parents at Bangor New Cemetery.

Threshin

James Fenton

[From *On Slaimish: An Ulster-Scots Collection* (James Fenton)]

Wuz a' soon an flail an flaff:
The sab an thrab o the Garvey,
Juntherin an jirgin
On cogged or glar-laired wheels;
The glancin jab an stoory flail o the forks,
Tossin the tirlin shaifs;
The flaff an flirry o the caff,
Doon-licht yella flakes –
But soon abain a', abain
Ivery soon in fiel or yaird or hoose,
A' ower the country an doon
The lang years:
The lang, hingin thrab an chokin sab,
The lachin squeals o weetchils,
Flailin their brenched sticks
Roon the hotchin staks,
The deein squeals
O leppin, clattin rats.

The en o a dream

James Fenton

[From *On Slaimish: An Ulster-Scots Collection* (James Fenton)]

Yin nicht, anither, an aye
That wie,
Tae thon nicht,
It come:
The plappin, getherin sugh frae
Oot the dark, tae
The hale lade ruz plowtin, plumpin, an
Frae oot the gowpin steam
He come:
Bak turned, heid booed
Bae the broo,
Claes blak an cattered, wat an reekied, an
The airm
Hel oot, the appen han
Waitin;
Tae the nicht the airm
Drapped, hingin jaist, an he come roon, then,
Lucked doon,
Een tae een; jaist luckin; an
Frae crinin scar
An the rivin stoon o seein an knowin
He'd ahlways
Knowed,
He lay gethered cowl in
The waitin dark.
It wud niver come that wie agane.

On Slaimish

An Ulster-Scots Collection

James Fenton

Oul Licht

& Other Ulster-Scots Poems

Philip Robinson

Hoose o Strae

Philip Robinson

[From *Oul Licht, & Other Ulster-Scots Poems*]

In, oot tha simmer sin,
Tha weefla rinnin wile
Tae Uncle Davie's hye-shade.
"Luk at thon,
Hae!"
Hale cairt-fu's o bales bigged heich.
Hye, or mebbe straa, or *strae*, wus it?
Uncle Davie cud tell ye
He'd a knowed oniehoo
Frae whut he wrocht theyeir,
Frae tha coorse taak o tha nighbers,
Frae his ain fiels an days
O puein, an plantin,
An cuttin.
He knowed tha seed an breed o thaim aa.

In, oot tha gowden sin,
Tha meeda's roastit gress
Tha coarnfiel's gaithert crap
Tae Uncle Davie's hye-shade.
Tha leevin proof
O iverie fairm,
Growein
Hootchin wi beese, wi gress, wi craps
Wi freens.
Iverie clump, thegither, wi tha yin root.

Iverie fiel a plantit tribe
O skailt seeds an tap breeds.
Ilka young blade
Pushin fur its ain place
In tha sin
Tae tha Reaper cum.

New bales noo bigged up
In giant steps
Stye
Up heich tae tha heid yins
Aa tha yin size, but, an poodher dry
Square as tha fiels,
Lake free-stane blocks, yella breeks
Bigged tha heicht o a hoose
Safe as hooses
Nae big bad wolf cud blaa
Uncle Davie's hoose o strae doon.
Fur him
A secret hidey-hole
A wee hut fur tha makkin
A wairm nest amang Uncle Davie's bales.
Boon tae be.

Davie wus lachin, fur his hoose wus slate't.
"Tha yin thaing aboot thaim balers noo –
Tha strae's nae uise fur thatchin".
Tha coarn stacks in tha fiels lang syne,
Wus thatch't forbye
Tha heid shaifs
On huts o coarn.
But noo tha strae
Aa push'd an beetle't tae a pulp

In a ticht-boon bale hel thegither wi stranglin twine
Ticht eneuch tae cut tha han
O a weefla no strang eneuch tae lift
A lifeless bale
Harp-strung wi hingman's raip.
Coontless dry banes o hairst, deid
Daen an dustit pushed dead
Square intae a machine.
Nae life noo
Apairt frae whut micht cum an
Mak its hame
Amang tha bales.

In, amang tha bales
Tha weefla stabs a tunnel.
Eneuch o an apenin jist
Fur ticht, draa'd in shoothers
Atween an up near tha tap
His ain wee hidlins hut
Big eneuch
Fur craalin in tae tha dairk
Wairm wame.

Anither warl, deep dairk in tha strae
Deep in his ain heid
Tha thocht o it
Hairt-liftin mystrie
Nae turnin bak, nae lukin bak
Nae licht, nae air
Huntin his past
Draims.
Hairt-stappin, heid turnin
Mooth shut agin tha stoor.

A weel-shewed button catched tha ticht twine.
Hans an elbas trap't forrit
Abane his shoothers
Wairm an ticht an dairk
Nae halie licht nor breath
O wun
Afore him noo.

A dug snorts in
Mair het air roon his anklers
Or a big bad wolf
Sweetin
Or tha deil hissel
Dairkenin tha dorr
Tha trap dorr
O this craalin hell-hole.

Jist twarthie fit awa
Ahint
Tae tha apen air
Whar tha halie spurit blaa's like tha wun,
Whar it wull,
Tae cries o danger.
"Loard, Get iz oot!"

Blin panic.
Nae air tae breathe
Nae air fur sweerin, mutterin
Or makkin prayers oot lood,
Nae point oniehoo
Gulderin
Intae this saft queeit moontain o deid
Empie ears.
"There's rats in thonner"
He mindit.

Elbas an airms an airse buckin an flailin
Tha strae
An tha deil in tha bales
Airsein oot
Shovin like buck mad.

Tae at lang last,
Oot
Free
Bak in tha lan
O tha leevin.
In tae tha apen air
Yinst mair.

Oot, in tha apen air
Dichtin wee bits o strae
Fae boggin claes.
Risin mair stour tae gar him blaa his neb.
Blak snatters, sair itchy een.
God
Nae lang'r mindit noo Uncle Davie cums up.
"Wud ye quat yer spittin", qu' he, *"whut's wrang?"*
Tha weefla apen't his tremmlin mooth,
"A wud gie oniethin tae get ma heid dunked in tha wattèr".

Tha weefla's blather wus near his een.
"Tha Meetin Hoose or tha lint hole?"
Davie axt, half coddin.
"Tha dam'll dae richtlie",
Dead serious.
"Ye'r aisie pleased. But mine", quo he,
"There's rats in thonner".

Davie knowed tha dunkin tha weefla needit
Afore tha Reaper cum.

Who Fears to Write of Ninety-Eight?

Stephen Dornan

Andrew James, *The Nabob: A Tale of Ninety-Eight*, notes and afterword by John Wilson Foster (Dublin: Four Courts Press, 2006)

In the opening line of an often quoted John Kells Ingram song, the speaker, with an implicit challenge, asks: "Who fears to speak of ninety-eight?" Writers, however, have tended not to be silent on the subject; if much blood was spilt in 1798, much ink was spilt in subsequent years in narrating and reimagining the events in literary texts. This tendency was notable across Ireland but took a distinctive turn in Ulster, where the focus was often on regional identity and dialect, in contrast to the Romantic Nationalism of Yeats's *Cathleen Ni Houlihan* (1902), or popular balladeers. Soon after the rising the Antrim poet and radical, James Orr, composed a vigorous Scots narrative poem, 'Donegore Hill'; an irreverent and sardonic view of the calamitous engagement from the perspective of a United Irish participant. The now obscure Ulster novelists John Gamble and James McHenry brought the events of ninety-eight to the pages of the historical novel through *Charlton* (1823) and *O'Halloran, or the Insurgent Chief* (1824) whilst later in the century W.G. Lyttle mythologised the story of *Betsy Gray, or hearts of Down* (1888). In the twentieth century the literary interest in ninety-eight continued; John Birmingham's *Northern Iron* (1907) is a notable text, whilst in the Troubles era writers such as Sam Hanna Bell and Scott Parker, amongst others, have

Badge of the Society of United Irishmen

returned to this period in their work. Fear has been undoubtedly been a conspicuous motif in these texts, but it is a fear that writers have felt compelled to confront in their literature.

One such writer was Andrew James, whose neglected collection of eight interweaved gothic tales has been repackaged as *The Nabob* for this edition. Andrew James was a pseudonym for Andrew

Strahan who, John Wilson Foster tells us in the afterword, was a notable Ulster lawyer with a keen interest in local history. The tales were initially published individually in *Blackwood's Edinburgh Magazine* from 1907, before being collected in 1911. Like much literature in Scots from Ireland, the tales have fallen into critical obscurity, and despite a recent upsurge in interest in, and funding for, Ulster-Scots culture, much of the best literature in the corpus remains out of print. In this context, the re-publication of *The Nabob* is a welcome development.

The first section of four tales is narrated in vernacular Scots to an anonymous editor, by an aged County Antrim schoolteacher whose father was involved in the action, which takes place in the build-up to and aftermath of the insurrection. These tales vividly evoke a dark and traumatised landscape, lacerated by internecine conflict and haunted by the victims of the brutal violence. Memorable and disturbing characters such as Galloper Starkie (the nabob of the title), the Last O'Hara, Davie Dunbar and the "Rid Man" are evoked vividly and endowed with the almost supernatural charisma of folk devils or folk heroes. The complex social, political and cultural allegiances and divided loyalties that the period elicited are incorporated into the narrative to good effect. The final four tales, set sixty years later and narrated in standard English, are ultimately less satisfactory aesthetically, although they are important in James's overall design.

The major achievement in this text undoubtedly lies in the opening four tales and the execution of the narrative of the schoolteacher, whose brooding, vernacular voice lends force to the horrific events that he recounts. James is certainly sensitive to local speech, in terms of lexicon, pronunciation and also the structure of oral delivery. For example, the school teacher begins his narrations in mid-conversation, twice with the syllable "No", which conveys the importance of accuracy for the narrator who seems to be correcting the inquisitive editor. James controls the digressive style and qualifying interjections of his narrator with skill. Much of the interest in these tales occurs in embedded commentary, opinion, reflection and anecdote which are often peripheral to the thrust of the central narrative.

John Wilson Foster's notes complement the text and provide useful historical background. In the afterword the reader is furnished with salient background information about this largely unknown author and useful interpretation of the tales. His insistence on reading the text through the prism of contemporary Northern Ireland, however, is the one problematic aspect of his commentary. It might be inviting to see the ghosts of ninety-eight resurrected in the bloodshed of Northern Ireland's dark recent past but in this instance it leads to unsatisfactory readings of the text. The idea of recurrence is undercut by the trajectory of the tales, which suggests progress. Thus the schoolteacher is an Ossianic figure, with dimming sight and a tendency to associate place with story. He is a repository of ephemeral local lore, and is poised on an historical threshold. Like Ossian, he is representative of a passing era and recognises the historical crisis he straddles. Commenting on cultural changes, he remarks that peoples' relation to their past is "a' changed now, mair parteecularly in the towns. Naebody there kens or cares who his great-grandfather was, or what he was" (46). The text, with a hint of nostalgia, suggests that the values, knowledge and dialect of the school teacher are becoming obsolete, but so too are the scars of ninety-eight fading. Consequently, James ultimately attempts to suggest an optimistic trajectory whereby the ghosts of ninety-eight are laid to rest and a natural order is restored with the ultimate return of MacDonnell in the second quartet of stories. The motif of return ultimately denotes resolution and closure rather than the incessant recurrence that Foster reads.

Despite the shortcomings of the second quartet of stories, the re-publication and repackaging of *The Nabob* is to be welcomed.

With this publication Andrew James can take his rightful place amongst those Ulster writers who dared to write of ninety-eight. This project was certainly not without its difficulties, and we get the sense that James empathises deeply with the schoolteacher's father, who in telling tales of the horror of ninety-eight "learned to thole it better; but ... till his dying day he couldna talk o' those awfu' times wi'out greeting." (35)

Taking of Ballymena market-house. A peasant placing a burning barrel against the door. From Ulster Journal of Archaeology, Second Series, Vol. I., No. 4, July, 1895.

Belfast, 2009

Stephen Dornan

I would build that dome in air,
That sunny dome! those caves of ice!
And all who heard should see them there,
And all should cry, Beware! Beware!'
(S.T. Coleridge)

Whaur the gumlie river Lagan barely
Flows o'er glaur; yin morn early
I took the notion, tae stop an ferly
At Belfast toon
In aa its gaudy grandeur rarely
Flooerin roon

Clocked on clabber, a tovey wheen,
New biggins glower wi gomerils' een
An a bleezin dome wi icy sheen
Chitterin bricht,
Shouders up aboon them clean
In skeenklin licht

Wi oxster strang a crane birls roon
Its load coagles i the lift aboon
Oor heids, then cleeks an noo the toon's
A wee mair built;
Whiles, forenent, a drill dirls doon
Through saft, saft silt

We maunna be fashed wi sleekit history,
The past's a dour auld whigmaleerie;
But this panorama o prosperity
Maun wairm oor hairts,
And ay wull bide tae shaw posterity
Oor unco pairts

Ilk lass an coof in fauncy gear
Weel turned oot they damn the fear,
O man nor baist but onwards steer
Wi oot regret;
The weans o noo on siller reared,
Can ocht forget

I doubt their likes would tak nae heed,
O a screed o blethers in a hauf-deid leid
An think it daft tae fash your heid
Wi dictionary
Hokin, an rhymes a body couldnae read
They're sae contrary

I wullnae fecht, I'd thole their gurns:
For Thomson, Orr an Robert Burns
I'll scrieve the Scotch that ghaistly yearns
For bygane times
An steer the sleekit jooks an turns
O Habbie's rhymes

Auld, crabbed wurds that arenae blate,
Tae getts begunk an glipes berate,
In squathries faa an sair bull-bait,
Spoutin invective;
Or sleekit, slee insinuate
Their ain perspective

I took the gate, tae clear my heid,
Awa fae tinsel trash and greed,
For fancy gear ah hae nae need
Nor public art:
Wameless sculptures dinnae bleed
An hae nae heart

I dandered aff through mony bleak
Streets, tae muckle waas, an keeked
Intil a graveyard, ahint a cleekit
Gate, whaur doon-deep
Aa throuither Belfast's faithers in oblique
Graves sleep

Thon yird is thrang wi mony banes,
Ablow the battered auld heidstanes
Daubed wi the blethers o glaiket weans,
Wha stroan and drink
Aboot the graves o them that's gane,
But ken, nor think

Wi wind in my hair, and licht in my een
I hoped oor scores were dichted clean,
But I in unco dwam hae seen
Thon dome uplift
Tae ding richt doon in smithereens:
A hailstane skift

Wee Davie Daylicht

Robert Tennant

[**Editor's note:** The following poem is a favourite of our Membership Secretary, Sally Young, who suggested that it be included in this issue of *Ullans*. Although the poem seems quite well known in the Ards, the only available information on Robert Tennant was obtained from the "Schuilwab", Scottish Language Dictionaries' interactive website in Scots for children and young people, now closed. This gave his dates of birth and death as 1830 and 1879 respectively.]

> Wee Davie Daylicht keeks owre the sea,
> Early in the morning, wi'a clear e'e;
> Waukens a' the birdies that are sleepin' soun',
> Wee Davie Daylicht is nae lazy loon.
>
> Wee Davie Daylicht glow'rs owre the hill,
> Glints through the greenwood, dances on the rill;
> Smiles on the wee cot, shines on the ha';
> Wee Davie Daylicht cheers the hearts o' a'.
>
> Come, bonnie bairnie, come awa' to me;
> Cuddle in my bosie, sleep upon my knee.
> Wee Davie Daylicht noo has closed his e'e
> In amang the rosy clouds, far ayont the sea.

Auld Daddy Darkness

James Ferguson

[**Editor's note:** In the course of searching for information on Robert Tennant, the following poem was found. No information on its author is to hand, and although from the text of these two poems there is an obvious borrowing of the "Davie Daylicht" concept it cannot be concluded with any certainty in which direction the borrowing occurred. The editor would be very pleased to hear from any member who can shed light on the details of the authors of either of these poems.]

Auld Daddy Darkness creeps frae his hole,
Black as a blackamoor, blin' as a mole:
Stir the fire till it lowes, let the bairnie sit,
Auld Daddy Darkness is no wantit yit.

See him in the corners hidin' frae the licht,
See him at the window gloomin' at the nicht;
Turn up the gas licht, close the shutters a',
An' Auld Daddy Darkness will flee far awa'.

Awa' to hide the birdie within its cozie nest,
Awa' to lap the wee flooers on their mither's breast,
Awa' to loosen Gaffer Toil frae his daily ca',
For Auld Daddy Darkness is kindly to a'.

He comes when we're weary to wean's frae oor waes,
He comes when the bairnies are getting aff their claes;
To cover them sae cozy, an' bring bonnie dreams,
So Auld Daddy Darkness is better than he seems.

Steek yer een, my wee tot, ye'll see Daddy then;
He's in below the bed claes, to cuddle ye he's fain;
Noo nestle to his bosie, sleep and dream yer fill,
Till Wee Davie Daylicht comes keekin' owre the hill.

Sysiphus: Or human Vanity

William Starrat

'Sysiphus, or Human Vanity', by 'W', is one of nine 'Scotch Poems' from the Laggan area of North-East Donegal that appeared in the *Ulster Miscellany* of 1753. William Starrat, ('W'), was a land surveyor and school-master from Strabane, and probably the principal editor and co-author of the *Ulster Miscellany*, along with 'M', (Rev. Matthew Draffen, Rector of Gartan, 1736-1785), and 'T' (Thomas Draffen, a land surveyor who worked mostly on the Abercorn estates in Tyrone, but lived in Lifford).

It was William Starrat, however, who had forged the earliest Ulster-Scots literary links with the great Scots poet Allan Ramsay, and whose *Tea-Table Miscellany, Or, A Collection of Choice Songs, Scots and English* was undoubtedly the inspiration for the *Ulster Miscellany*. Indeed, the seventh 'Scotch Poem' in the *Ulster Miscellany* was a pointed 'An additional Verse to the Widow my Laddie'. The original 'Widow my Laddie' had just been published by Allan Ramsay in his *Tea-Table Miscellany* in 1750. But thirty years earlier, William Starrat had sent a manuscript to Ramsay of another Scotch poem: 'A Pastoral in Praise of Allan Ramsay', annotated "Straban May 15th 1722". In Ramsay's own hand a note was added: "Mr Starrat Teaches Mathematicks at Straban." Starrat's poem was published in 1725 as a broadsheet, "A Pastoral in Praise of Allan Ramsay By Willy Starrat", and Starrat's poem appears in most versions of the collected works of Allan Ramsay, along with a poetic response from Ramsay which effectively dubbed him the 'Bard of Crochan'.

William Starrat was better known as a surveyor and mathematician than as a schoolmaster or poet. He was one of the foremost land surveyors in Ireland, mostly active between 1716 and 1738, with major estate surveys completed for important landlords in counties Armagh, Donegal, Fermanagh, Londonderry, Leitrim, Cavan, Antrim and Tyrone. In 1723 he was made a freeman of Lifford, County Donegal, just across the bridge from Strabane where he owned several properties including his schoolhouse, in which he taught Arithmetic, Algebra and Geometry. The only book published under his own name appeared in 1733 dedicated to the 'Provost and Fellows of Trinity College, Dublin' and was a mathematical treatise: *The Doctrine of Projectiles*. Significantly, among the lengthy list of distinguished mathematicians and military 'subscribers' was one "Mr. Allan Ramsay, Edinburgh".

In Greek mythology SISYPHUS was punished for his selfish craftiness and deceit by being forced to roll an immense boulder up a hill, only to watch it come back to hit him, repeating this action for eternity. William Starrat's poem here is a satire on pride and ambition, driving an "… aspiring *cheel* [youth], Wha wad to wealth and grandeur *speel* [climb]; Wha uses a' his art, and skill To *row* [roll] his *meentith* [vain glory] up the hill".

Philip Robinson

SYSIPHUS: *Or human Vanity*

I Pity the aspiring cheel,
Wha wad to wealth, and grandeur speel;
Wha uses a' his art, and skill
To row his meentith up the hill:
For when he gains the highest ground,
Nae resting-place will there be found;
He will (as ithers oft hae priev'd)
Of a' his rowth be quickly reev'd:
For death, or fate, it maksna whither,

Ne'er lets them bide o'erlang the gither;
But as the righteous Judge thinks fit,
Takes it frae him, or him frae it.
And when enjoyment's past and gane,
Remembrance gi's him unco pain.
The mair he priz'd his former state,
The mair he grieves when driv'n frae't.
What dolours fill the weary wight,
When tumbled frae his artfu' hight?
Nor yet will his example fear
Anither, or his moilings mar:
He scrambles up the self same track,
Sae wins the top, sae tumbles back.
Thus *Sysiphus* wi' mony a grane,
Up the steep bevil heeves his stane:
The summit gain'd, 'twill no stand still,
But headlang trumbles down the hill:
Again he upwards warks the stane,
And it comes trumpling down again.
Did some of the celestial pow'rs
Luick down on this doyl'd wark o' ours
They'd form their judgments o' us thus:
That a' mankind's ae *Sysiphus*.——W.

My meentith an' me

Alan Millar

My meentith an' me: a salutary tale (aiblins)

Featuring the author and another from the Ards Peninsula

> *I pity the aspiring cheel,*
> *Wha wad to wealth, and grandeur speel;*
> *Wha uses a' his art, and skill*
> *To row his meentith up the hill*
>   William Starrat, Strabane, 1753

PAIRT YIN

My meentith rests on Croachan Hill,
Surveys Strabane like bardic Bill,
The hind who ainst did scrieve his fill
On Sisyphus
The Greek; wi' Ulster-Scots an' quill
An' little fuss!

Me an' my meentith speeled thegeither,
Frae Lifford brig in oddest weather,
Sweetin' hard for he's nae feather
An' country rare;
For wance he's up, there's nae known tether
Will keep him there!

On twitchy meentith I maun haste,
Tae pen my thoughts an' mak the maist,

O' this brief time to scrieve the baste,
For ilka quiver
Could be the thing that starts the chase
Bak tae the river ...

PAIRT TWA

My canny meentith's high aboon,
A corbie craw that flies aroon,
My fragile heart an' grounded shoen,
On sleekit warl;
Keeps bak the gype, the coof an' loon,
Wad vex his carle.

My boorish meentith is the champ,
That steers me throu' the social swamp,
Gaes muckle wans, the 'eejit' stamp,
The borin' fools
Whose witterin's gaes lugs the cramp,
The walkin' mouls.

My waeful meentith sharps his stakes,
Agin' ilka form progression takes,
Ilk bonnie plan he ay forsakes
As futures foe;
An' disavows what reason makes,
Wi' resounding NO!

My de'ilish meentith is a yoke,
Dis snoke an' scobe an' rutted hoke,
An' slink awa frae ither folk,
Tae bae naw wise;
Lays thrapple thick wi' churning boke,
An' poortith cries.

PAIRT THREE

My Springer meentith sudden strains,
An' surges farrit agin' his reins,
The testy 'hind' o' a' terrains
Keeks oore the bru,
Tae see what awfu' sight pertains,
We'll heddie rue!

A stane slow speels up Croachan's swards,
Hard heaved by yin withoot regards,
For onything but dogged yards,
Wi' heels dug in;
Lord abeen, it's the man frae Ards
It's R—n!

Man an' meentith come tae savor,
An' ha'e a bonnie cryptic claver
In Laggan Scots wi a' its flavor
Fair fie, I ca'
Come sit a while an' haver
Aboot Donega'.

The Doctor staps an' mops his brow,
Trigs as weel as airms allow,
"This cursed thing's a muckle sow,"
He grim confides;
Then asks a han' on up the knowe –
Which I oblige …

Straight awa my meentith trumbles,
Doon the hill he wildly rumbles,
I mak fareweel in 'sorry' mumbles
Tae "P—l" in haste,

Then aff tae Lifford brig in tumbles,
Oh what a waste.

Postscript

Twa meentiths lay near Croachan fit,
Ne'er speeled the hill fur wurnie fit,
'Cause ilka ane judged the sunny sit
The best o' selves;
Just 'trumphery' sat an' what o't,
Sic happier elves.

The Gellick

Stephen Dornan

Ah bide in neuks the lee-lang day
An rear my thrangs o weans away
Fae comfort, heat an licht o day
Sprattlin in clart,
Whaur ceevilisation halds nae sway,
Nor polished art.

You dinnae like tae think Ah'm here,
Aboot your sonsy, fauncy gear
An gin you see me sprattlin near
It's batterin broom,
Or stampin shoon, I doubt an fear
Will seal my doom.

Ah'll exercise my muckle hooks
Amang your claes an unread books,
An stick my neb at nicht fae neuks
Crawlin and creepin;
Then, wi steady feet and furtive jooks,
Ah'll find you sleepin!

Doon yer lug hole Ah'll come dashin,
Borin, burrowin, batterin, bashin
Hokin, wigglin, garravashin,
Intil yer heid
An lae you sneezin, pechin, fashin,
Wi oot remead.

Like an ammonite concealed in stane,
Ah'll curl richt up and bide my lane
Atween your gullet and your brain
An hibernate;
Ah'll dormant bide until your pain
Micht dissipate.

Like an arraheid ablow the glaur
Or a peat-choked body buried far
Ablow a bog Ah've unco power,
Like artefact or relic;
An whan Ah twitch sic wurds Ah'll gar
Boke fae your bake as "gellick!"

Whar is Campbell?

Alan Millar

S everal years ago, whilst satisfying a bout of intense curiosity
to find out more about the early Ulster-Scots poets of east
Antrim, I found the door of retired farmer and well-known local
historian Mr Ernest McAllister Scott of Ballyeaston. I first become
aware of Ernie and his connection with this tradition of writing
from his involvement in the 1992 book *The Country Rhymes of
Samuel Thomson*, the weaver poet who hailed from Carngranny,
just a few miles away. One of the things Ernie told me, that single
time we met, was that James Campbell (1759 to 1818), the Bard
of Ballynure, was buried in Ballynure old graveyard. It wasn't until
a year later that I went to the graveyard looking for Campbell. I
was moved to write this poem when, after having failed to find
him, I discovered Ernie Scott newly buried there himself.

> In Ballynure lies a plot o' banes,
> Thranged wi' weeds; an' faded names,
> On forgotten rows o' foggy stanes,
> Frae ither times,
> Whar muckle kinfolk left remains,
> An' chanted rhymes.
>
> Whar is Campbell the plebs 'Magog'?
> We scan the stanes an' scratch the fog,
> For Ballynure's eydent modest cog
> O' poetic art;
> Who scribed awee on loom side log
> Wi' furious heart.

Lang time syne his bouk was sent,
Tae this groun' wi' stanes asklent;
Frae Ballybracken; by lane an' bent
An' final loanen,
The twelve shank timmer breekum went,
Slowly wendin'.

Sic funeral thrangs at Campbell's grave,
The weaver Bard, the honest knave;
Yet so fragile was the memory saved
In 'posey's' book,
That on this chiel nae critic raved,
Or felt to look.

Which aule gressy kirk-yard bump,
Was ainst the Bardic burial hump?
O' Jim, who skelped the rotten rump
Wi' nae amends,
O' rich folks greed in stanza's plump,
Tae poortith friends.

Big man o' liberty an' wee,
A 'minor' poet, full o' Paine was he;
This wabster chiel kent a' men free –
Naturally;
His struggles led tae you an' me –
Politically.

Aiblins baith Orr an' Thomson threw
Their e'en across this kirk-yard view,
Spoke words wi' Jim, grave an' few,
On some poor de'il,
Whose race o' life fled oore the bru,
For want o' meal.

Then tae the Tap Room in the rain,
Tae prie't an' crack wi' loud refrain,
Sing bawdy songs an' sangs o' pain –
The tappin' shoen,
O' bards an' cotters pish't at e'en,
A drunken boon.

Oh country craft wi' powers rare
Flit me thro' a space time tear,
Tae Beattie's Tap Room, Ballyclare
Twa hunner year ago;
Wi' bearded Campbell seated there
Chattin' hoarse an' low?

Wi' fancies e'en I see his shifts,
'Twixt stool an' tap he deftly flits,
Gleg an' canny wi' simpler wits,
He cracks wi' gypes,
An' odd time slams the rich man's writs,
The poor man's fykes.

Then pries a drap an' sings a verse,
'Expostulating' whiskey's curse.
In Corbie tones, mock morose,
Agin malted vial,
Warns ilka young een frae a dose,
O 'Campbell's Cordial'.

Wi' sky clear e'en, an cheekums flushed
Oot his 'Night Cap' comic rushed;
Then 'Mullan's Adieu' dainty pushed,
Its liltin' mode,
Has burly tap men unco hushed,
Till cheers explode.

Fornenst him now, an' oiled on rum,
I bid him polite, his life tae plumb;
Lay pipe an' pot atap the lum
An' sing tae me,
Abeen the revelers bee scap hum,
His life awee.

Canny Campbell gaed a chuckle –
"I'll for you my heed unbuckle
For bardship is the soul o' muckle"
He says to me,
"Oblige yer ain tae final ruckle
For sic are thee."

"My trade is wabster, slave o' dree,
A family man, an' boozer tae,
Wi' Masonic rites I full agree,
'Lucubration'
Square an' gauge were gaed tae me,
In Bal'easton.

"I endless weave the flat entrail,
Knot snappit warp wi' chippit nail,
Feed skirlin' weans on watered kail,
A waeful dish;
I fyke for meat, an' bitter rail
An' fervent wish.

"For next my loom my inkpot stands,
My shuttle thrown wi' blotted hands
As first an' fierce my blow it lands,
In thinkin' hurly,
Afore I dam corruption's bands,
In written fury.

"I curse all Lords an' pray they writhe,
Wi' Prelates bloated frae the tithe,
In penitent agony; still alive
Aflame in hell,
Wi' meal monger's lapping lithe,
Oore fiery dell.

"Maist times I fairer themes embrace:
Tae fond recall a parted face
In epitaph; or aiblins address
'The porky pig';
Sing sangs for poor folk aft in stress,
At soiree's big.

"On politics I aft times gabble,
In secret oaths I ainst did dabble,
Stood 'United' wi' poortith 'rabble';
A vow I swore,
I rose agin' the monied cabal,
At Donegore.

Ach, revolution's a bitter tale
Tae raise a flag; then watch it fail.
For liberty I was coped in jail,
Wi' not a steek;
Near Antrim town we turned on tail,
For Slemish Peak!

"Yet mind the 'Titan' Tammy Paine –
I wrote awee for his tombstane,
Twa hunner lines in verses plain
O' tribute fine,
His 'Rights o' Man' nae slur shall stain,
Neither yours nor mine."

"Jim yer right" I butt in sharp
"Bonds twixt times are tight as warp;
Be it Hand or Crown or Star or Harp,
Afore the vote,
The granny's granny o' them that carp
Milked a goat!"

I saw the Campbell's color alter,
His mou' contort, his patter falter,
"Your nae chiel in this warls halter,"
He groans aloud,
"But madness come frae Bacchus altar –
The whiskey bauld."

Hitchin' breeks he pulls thegeither –
"Ainst again my boozy blether,"
Has gart my heed a' throuither,"
He tells himself,
"Awa hame ye ghaistly ither,"
Ye sleekit elf."

Wi' this his yarn o' life went lame,
Frae Beattie's back I sharply came,
Stood stung fornenst a fogless stane,
In twenty ten –
For on it scrieved a different name,
By modern han'.

Shocked to see, an' freshly happed,
An earthly mound the shovel slapped,
Set wi' wreaths in ribbons wrapped,
For Ernest Scott,
Who since we met, his journey stapped,
At this 'mad' spot!

I mind his farmer's studied air,
Judge my grasp o' dialect 'fair';
Thon single hour we briefly shared,
In Bal'easton.
I heard Jim's story, rhymes an' mair –
Country wisdom!

Oore search concludes o' chiseled names,
Nae sic, amang the foggy stanes,
Ca'd Campbell in this plot o' banes;
The bard forgot –
How little o' his tale remains,
O' sic a lot?

Somewhar here his singin' banes,
Rest wi' countless staneless ither bein's,
Yet still his wabster yarn remains –
In words he wrought,
That scudded throu' the veins,
O' Ernie Scott!

An' Ernie Scott, wan warp o' monie,
Fired, I ween, my needful habbie,
Tae weave the life o' Campbell canny;
An' grasp the roots,
O' makkin rhymes, like famous Rabbie,
An' scrievin beuks.

Now Jim an' Ernie scud the ether,
Baith in twilight a' thegeither,
'Neath Ballynure wi' worms an' clabber;
What do they say?
Prie the gill an' yarn forever;
Or poetic lay?

Dailygone

J.S.

[The following was submitted to the *Northern Whig* newspaper in 1924 by a 'J.S.']

Sir, – In the current issue of the "Whig" some letters have appeared on "Ulster Words and Phrases." One correspondent mentions the word "Dailygone." Some years ago there lived in Coreen, Braid Valley, a Mr. Andrew M'Bride, schoolmaster, who was a contributor in prose and verse to the local paper. One poem he wrote was entitled "Dailygone," and I think that since Alexander Anderson (the surfaceman) wrote the famous poem "Bairnies Cuddle Doon" no better poem than Mr. M'Bride's has appeared in the same dialect. I append the first verse:—

Dailygone.

As Phœbus and his tired steeds
    Gang doon the western braes,
And Nicht keeks ower the east wa-heids
    Cled in his darksome claes,
The birds flee up and dicht their nebs,
    And bees buzz to their bykes,
And spiders lee their half-spun webs
    'Mang whins or holes or dykes —
      At Dailygone.

— Yours, &c.,

J.S.

Carnmoney Witches

Philip Robinson

The following is an extract from the *Belfast Commercial Chronicle*, on 20 September 1807:

"At Carnmoney, Friday last, (14 September) Mr Alexander Montgomery, aged 60, to Miss Henderson, aged 16. Montgomery's former wife died on the 19th ult. by suffocation occasioned by Mary Butter's incantations".

Handwritten below is the information, "Mary Butter was the celebrated Carnmoney witch".

The following was transcribed from the *UJA*, 1908, Vol. XIV, pp. 35–37:

A NEW SONG CALLED;
CARMONEY WITCHES;
　　To which are added,
Large Glasses full to the Brim,
　　And the Protest.
Printed in memory of witch-craft 1808.

CARMONEY WITCHES
A humorous modern Song, founded on fact,
　　by F. B.—, Cumber, Granshaw.
Tune — "Lovely Molly has an air —"

In Carrick town a wife did dwell,
Who does pretend to conjure witches
Auld Barbara Goats and lucky Bell,
Ye'll no lang to come through her clutches;
A waefu' trick this wife did play,
On simple Sawney, our poor tailor,
She's mittimiss'd the other day
To lie in limbo with the Jailor:
This simple Sawney had a Cow
Was aye as sleekit as an otter
It happen'd for a month or two,
Aye when they churn'd they got nae butter;
Roun-tree tied in the Cow's tail,
And vervain glean'd about the ditches;
These freets and charms did not prevail,
They cou'd not banish the auld witches:
The neighbour wives a' gather'd in
In number near about a dozen,
Elfpie Dough and Mary Linn,
An' Keat M'Cart the tailor's cousin,
Aye they churn'd an' aye they swat,
Their aprons loos'd and coost their mutches
But yet nae butter they could get,
They blest the Cow but curst the witches:
Had Sawney summoned all his wits,
And sent awa for Huie Mertin,
He could have gall't the witches guts
An' cur't the kye to Nannie Barton;
But he may show the farmer's wab
An' lang wade through Carmoney gutters,
Alas! it was a sore mis-jab
When he employ'd auld Mary Butters;
The sorecerest open'd the scene,

With magic words of her invention,
To make the foolish people keen
    Who did not know her base intention,
She drew a circle round the churn,
    An' wash'd the staff in south run water
An' swore the witches she would burn,
    But she would have the tailor's butter.
When sable night her curtain spread,
    Then she got on a flaming fire,
The tailor stood at the cow's head
    With his turn'd waistcoat in the byer;
The chimney cover'd with a scraw,
    An' ev'ry crevice where it smoak'd,
But long before the cock did craw
    The people in the house were choak'd,
The muckle pot hung on all night
    As Mary Butters had been brewing,
In hopes to fetch some witch or wight
    Whas entrails by her art was stewing
In this her magic a' did fail
    Nae witch or wizard was detected;
Now Mary Butters lies in jail,
    For the base part that she has acted.
The tailor lost his son an' wife,
    For Mary Butters did them smother
But as he hates a single life,
    In four weeks time he got another;
He is a cruse auld canty chiel,
    An' cares nae what the witches mutters
He'll never mair employ the deil,
    Not his auld agent, Mary Butters;
At day the tailor left his post,
    Though he had seen no apparation

Nae wizard grim nae witch nor ghost,
Though still he had a strong suspicion
That some auld wizard wrinkled wife,
Had cast her cantrips o'er poor brawney
Cause she and he did live in strife,
An' whare's the man can blame poor Sawney;
Wae sucks for our young lasses now,
For who can read their mystic matters
Or tell if their sweet hearts be true,
The folk a run to Mary Butters;
To tell what thief a horse did steal,
In this she was a mere pretender
An' has nae art to raise the deil
Like that auld wife, the witch of Endor
If Mary Butters be a witch,
Why but the people all should know it,
An' if she can the muses touch
I'm sure she'll soon descry the poet,
Her ain familiar ass she'll sen'
Or paughlet wi' a tu' commission,
To pour her vengeance on the men,
That tantalises her condition.

The following, from M'Skimmin's *History of Carrickfergus*, contributes an explanation:

"At the spring assizes at Carrickfergus, March, 1808, Mary Butters, Carrickfergus, was put forward on the charge of witchcraft. The Belfast News-letter of Friday, the 21st August, 1807, notes: A melancholy event took place on Tuesday night in the house of Alexander Montgomery, tailor, at Carnmoney Meeting House. Montgomery, it appears, had a cow which continued to give milk as usual, but of late no butter could be produced from the milk. An opinion, which had been too long entertained by many people in the country, was unfortunately instilled into the mind of Montgomery's wife, that whenever such circumstances occurred, it was occasioned by the cow having been bewitched. In this opinion she was fortified by the concurring testimony of every old woman in the parish, each of whom contributed her story of what she had seen and known in former times.

At length the family were informed of a woman named Mary Butters, who resided at Carrickfergus. They accordingly went to her, and brought her to their house, for the purpose of curing the cow. It is not known what stratagems she employed to work her pretended enchantment, but the house had a strong sulphureous smell, and on the fire was a large pot in which were some milk, needles, pins, and crooked nails. Montgomery's wife, son, and an old woman named Margaret Lee were suffocated, but Mary Butters, the sorceress, being thrown out on a dunghill, where she received some hearty kicks, soon after recovered, and was sent to Carrickfergus jail. At the inquest held on the 16th August, at Carnmoney, on the bodies of Elizabeth Montgomery, David Montgomery, and Margaret Lee, the jury stated that they came by their death from suffocation, occasioned by a woman named Mary Butters, in her making use of some noxious ingredients, in the manner of a charm, to recover a cow, the property of Alexander Montgomery. At the assizes, Mary Butters, the witch of Carnmoney, was discharged by proclamation".

Thochts thaut A hae

Charlie 'Tha Poocher' Rannals

A wus sittin tha ither dey tryin tae keep tha sun oot o mae een whun a thocht rin through mae heid. Noo am naw sae sure if that is a guid thing but here it is onywye.

A think oor Ullans tongue needs tae bae spake mair oot amang tha wider community. Noo what is he channerin on aboot A hear yese ax? Weel its lake this here, A hae absarved whiles whun yins wha taak naethin but Ullans at hame whun they ir oot aboot ither places wud stert taakin soarta English. If they ir interviewed on tha wireless ir tha lake, they slide intae a mair 'polite vocabulary' an forget thaur ain mither tongue.

Noo, tha rayson for thaut micht bae that they hae bane mis-caa'ed aa thaur deys bae tha yins in tha educashun wurl, wha seem tae ken mair nir tha rest o is. They ir affronted tae spake thaur ain tongue for fear o maakin themsels luk lake gomeys.

Noo, maesel A'm as bad as tha rest for A hae nae bother taakin mae ain tongue whun am amang mae North Entrim freens. But shame on me, tha minute A hit Cuilren a graet change comes ower mae, an heth, if A dinnae stert taakin English tha wye tha toon yins taak. Then aff coorse whiles if ye hard mae telephone tongue ye wud think A wus oot o Eton college.

A cannae unnerstan tha rayson for this for A hae absarved that it seems tae bae jest tha Ullans taakers wha dae this. Wae seem tae bae tha yins wha haetae change – why? Aff coorse thaur is a wheen o guid folk, mine ye they ir licht on the grun, wha taak tha Ullans tongue nae odds whaur they ir. A taak mae kep aff tae them for they ir proud o thaur native tongue an the rest o is wull hae tae learn frae them.

Becaase, its tha only wye that rest o the wurl wull taak heed o is an see that wae hae a tongue o wur ain an that wur naw feart tae use it. It wull fair shut up tha yins wha sae that they niver hard tha Ullans tongue an kan only help keep oor tongue leevin. Aff coorse A mann maak a stert maesel an try an spake tha wye A ocht tae, tha wye mae ain yins in North Entrim spake.

Gie is aa tha chance tae taak lake wae dae,
It daes naeboady nae herm, thats what A sae
Sure its naw a crime, an ye'll naw get hung
Houl up yer heid an spake yer ain Ullans tongue.

May 2017

[Editor's note: It's a pleasure to welcome back an Aul Freen to the pages of *Ullans,* with a cry from the heart that our readers will heartily endorse.]

Tha Killaughey Smiddie

Wilbert Magill

In a place that's caa'd Killaughey,
 There wus a smithie o great fame,
He wus tha best at shoddin horses,
 an Bab Mairtin wus his name.
Tha fairmers cum fae miles aroon,
 tae hae thair horses shod,
It gien them a firm fittin,
 as in tha fiels the'd plod.

Tha big Clydesdales an Ayrshires,
 wud line up an wait thair turn,
An efter eatin oot thair nosebag,
 wud drink oot o tha burn.
But time noo shair it changes things,
 fae whut it uise tae be,
Nae mair dae ye hear tha anvil.
 ringin oot, dum … diddle … dee.

Tha Smiddie it's still stannin,
 but tha dorrs is boultit ticht,
An tha fire it went oot ye see,
 it's nae mair burnin bricht.
Tha anvil… ay… it's quait noo,
 nae mair hemmers on it faa,
An tha Bellas irnae warkin,
 shair this is ivver aa.

Tha lum is nae mair reekin,
    as it did in days o yore,
An Bab's oul leather apern,
    is on a nail ahint tha dorr.
Ye see there's nae mair need fur horses
    fur tae pu tha pue ye ken,
It's daen noo wi tha Trecter,
    ay… Progress is tae blame.

Tha Killhoose Dances

Wilbert Magill

Shair Kerdur is a quait wee place,
    on weekdays apairt fae yin,
But on Setterday nicht it cums tae life,
    whun tha velye jist begins.
In a place that's caa'd tha Killhoose,
    that's whar they houl tha dance,
An fae echt o'clock tae midnicht,
    they aa jump aboot an prance.

Tha fowk aa cum fae far an wide,
    an roon aboot A declare,
An them that cannae get inside
    jist dance in tha apen air.
Tha lassies the'll aa stan aroon,
    on yin side o tha flair,
Lukkin strecht across tha hoose
    at tha men fowk hoo ir there.

But listen an A'll tell ye,
    aboot tha tither nicht,
Fur A niver noo saa sic a sicht,
    an A lached wi aa ma micht.
Big Bertha, she's fae Hoarnie's Neuk,
    an bigged lake Despert Dan,
She ayewyes haes tae sit an luk,
    fur she cannae get a man.

She weers aff tha shoother dresses,
    wi twa pleats up each side,
An wi her hab-nail bits on,
    bates tha flair an keeps in time.
But this nicht noo it wus differn't,
    fur wee Tamas John wus there,
He leeves ahint tha Lower Ludge,
    an haes a wudden leg fur shair.

Tha M.C. he got oarder,
    as on tha pletfoarm he wud stan,
Tha nixt dance is tha ladies choice,
    mak shair ye git yer man.
Fer we'r dancin tha Gay Gordens,
    an whun A gie ye tha sign,
Rin quick an get yer pairtners,
    an then foarm twa strecht lines.

He shouted oot noo… yin… twa… three
    an they aa tuk aff rael fast,
An they aa got thair pairtners,
    but Big Bertha… she wus last.
She then lukked doon at Tamas John
    an sayed, jist cum wi me,
She wus tha proodest wummin in tha place,
    an her een lit up wi glee.

Then tha Fiddlers they got stairtit,
    tha Gordens fur tae play,
An as they danced aroon tha flair
    Bertha haed this tae say.
Tamas wull ye pit yer airms aroon me,
    an haud on noo real ticht,
It'll sin be time fur birlin
    … haud on wi aa yer micht.

Noo wi tha hoochin an tha clappin,
   an tha stampin on tha flair,
The yins that cudnae git inside,
   cum tae tha wundaes fur tae stare.
Then tha yins inside stap't dancin,
   as Big Bertha tuk tha lead,
An liftin Tamas by tha peg,
   houled him up abin her heid.

She stairtit fur tae birl him,
   but it wus tha wrang wye roon,
Whun Tamas's wudden leg spun aff,
   an they fell doon tae tha groon.
Noo... tha moral tae tha weemin fowk,
   fae Big Bertha's this ye see,
Whun ye gan oot tae tha dancing
   Dinnae en up lake me.
Fur A got sae excited
   an wus sae fu o glee,
An didnae ken that A wus coortin
   hauf a man an hauf a tree.

Portavogie Crack

Elaine Amy Orr McFeeters

The Wee White Wuman

A lang time ago there wur a terble lot o springs an wals aroon Portavogie. The maist infamus wal is the Queen's Wal where legen hus it the "wee white wuman" can be seen.

Before the 2nd Worl War the Bog Road hud a quer load o fairms on it an this wuman fa'd a toss in the deep snow, cudnae get up an deed. Her ghost can be seen [or her presence felt] fae time tae time.

Keep an ee oot for her.

Ma Da telt me this story …

Lang before the ferry, lorries travelled fae Ardglass by Newton tae Poravogie tae the fish auctions.

Yin foggy nicht, drivin hame on the Bog Road, yin o these lorry drivers hut somethin at the Queen's Wal.

He got oot tae check whit wuz wrang … an felt icy hans on the back o his neck.

But there wuz naethin there … He got back in his cab, drove hame an NIVER took the Bog Road way hame again.

Sae the neext time ye're drivin doon there, in the dark, as ye pass whar the wal wuz, juust check in yer rear view mirror … just in case she's in the back sate!!! Or if ye'r walkin there yersel aye look oot for her walkin beside ye. Ye'll know al aboot it for ye'll be wile coul.

A hae mine o the wal there wi a great big wudden trap dor, an mibbe the story o the wee white wuman wuz a deterrent tae weans in case they fell intae the wal. But mibbe no … ye niver know … Sae watch yersel gaun doon there in the dark noo!!

Hae ye mine?

If ye leeved in Portavogie in the '60s ye'll hae mine o aa these! Whan A wuz a wee lass we aye went doon the warren tae the san pits an jumped aff the tap tae see wha cud lan the farthest an be the wunner. Oor feet wur kilt! Then we went doon the shore for a sweem. We hudnae ony big folk wi us but we were aa richt … nane o us got droont.

Sometimes we walked tae the Green isle just for fun whan the tide wuz oot. We wur aye telt tae "mine the burn". Noo an again we got a lift back on the trailer o a tractor belangin tae Jimmy Limon. A think he wuz getherin wreck for the gairden. Doon the warren wuz bits o swamps fu o newts an frogs. We hud quer times. We used tae gether bracken an mak wee hooses. We gethered stuff fae the shore an the oul dump doon the warren. Sometimes we fun banes o coos an horses tae. There's hooses there noo.

Doon at Hubert's dump whar the Quays is noo, the gypsies used tae camp in oul horse drawn caravans. The swingin boats came tae the warren tae. There wuz hoopla an dodgems an a wheen o ither stalls. There wuz a wee show that cum ivery year where a the water is noo on the New Harbour Rd. Quer times indeed.

Big steam rollers fixed the road, an whun it wuz wairm the tar melted an we got it on oor legs an sandals. Oor Mas took it aff wi butter. There used tae be a hoose called Happy Days doon the Cloughey Road at the en o Broon's Loanen. It wuz aye buzzin wi folk. Ma Da telt me there wuz that monny folk in it they took it in turns tae go tae bed!! Loads o folk stayed in Portavogie in the Summertime, maistly fae Bulfast. The sun aye seemed tae be shinin an we played ootside aa day. Mibbe got a piece o plain breid an butter dipped in shugger tae keep us goin til we got oor denner.

Annie Mary Coffey leeved doon the Cloghey Road an she hud a dug an a wheen o cats. She wuz a luvly wumman. Joe Tampsin hud a big white horse cald Johnny an he used tae be the horse that led the procession at the Twalth. We used tae play hop scotch an build guiders wi oul pram wheels an a wudden fish box. We played chasin an hide an seek thru the warren. We pedalled all over on oor bikes cos the roads wurnae busy. Naebody worried aboot us even if we were away for hoors.

We niver hud ony bother sleepin then! Hae ye mine?

The freen who almost kilt me

Brian Chestnutt

There was a time when he was mine;
We aiftan taaked alane.
Used tae hule each up at night,
Wey maistly half a brain.

Nithin we cunny tak about –
We were always on a par,
Lovin every second,
Always in a bar.

Aw the greens we used tae see there;
Crack always the best;
Enjoyed every minute;
Cared nithin boot the rest.

Aw how we use tay laugh and joke.
We made each ooer think;
But we never seen this coming,
Baith heeded fer the brink.

Cas fer every glaase that I sut doon,
A was moving mare away
Fray awl the freens and femily
That I had wance yin day.

Noo I dinny see him any mare.
Hope he never caws;
An a wish I'd never met him,
That evil alcohol.

Noo I'll naw tell yae nae lies;
I dae still tae this day,
Aboot the freen that almost kilt me
... He's never far away ...

John Getty of Randalstown and Ballymena (1781-1857): Ulster-Scots Scholar and Writer

Philip Robinson

John Getty from Ballytresna, beside the River Maine near Randalstown (1781-1857), was a Ballymena schoolmaster who first comes to our notice in 1804. James Orr's *Poems on various subjects* was published in that year, and among the names of the subscribers appeared that of 'J. Geddis, Ballytresna' ('Geddis' and 'Geddes' are older Scots forms of the 'Getty' surname).

Two years later, James Orr of Ballycarry published a poem in the *Belfast Commercial Chronicle* that struck a particular local chord with Getty. It was called 'Gracehill. The Moravian Settlement near Ballymena' (*Belfast Commercial Chronicle,* 14 May 1806). Within a few weeks, John Getty had penned and published—in the same paper—a poetic tribute: 'Stanzas Addressed to J. O. On Reading his Poem on Gracehill' (*Belfast Commercial Chronicle*, 9 June 1806). He hailed Orr as 'Ultonia's Genius', reflecting the line in 'Gracehill' where Orr had written, 'The genius of the [River] Main uprais'd his head'. Getty's poem opens with a Latin dedication to Orr ('a poet is born, not made'), and proceeds to identify himself as the mouthpiece of the 'Genius of the Main'. In the final verse, John Getty would have Orr awake again his 'sounding lyre' and called on Ultonia [Ulster]'s Genius to inspire 'your deathless verses':

STANZAS ADDRESSED TO J[ames]. O[rr].—
ON READING HIS POEM ON GRACEHILL.

"Poeta nascitur non fit"

Sweet Poet, Nature's artless child,
As ever wak'd the soothing strain.
With joy I hear thy "wood-notes wild,"
Resound along our jocund plain:
Enraptur'd with poetic flame,
Methinks I see thee strike the lyre,
And hail the *Genius of the Main*,*
A deathless sonnet to inspire.

[*The River Main runs past Gracehill, and after describing a number of beautiful meanders, falls into Lough Neagh, a little below Randalstown, in Earl O'Neill's deer park.—'G']

Return and view the happy place,
So worthy thy harmonious lay;
Together, let us fondly trace
What Gracehill's lovely scenes display;
Whose Sons pursue fair Virtue's way.
Adorn'd with science, truth and sense;
Whose Daughters shame the blushing day
For blooming youth and innocence.

We'll seek yon fragrant rosy bow'r,
Where Nature's charms are full display'd;
Or court fair Virtue's soothing pow'r,
Beneath the milk-white hawthorn shade;
Or wander in some lonely glade
Along the winding banks of Main,
Till night, in sable smiles array'd,
Resumes her solitary reign.

In converse sweet, we'll pass the time,
And Learning's many paths explore;
Or view Creation's works devine,
And talk their various wonders o'er;
And learn, with rev'rence to adore,
That Great uncomprehensive Mind,
Which call'd from *nought* the boundless store
Of *beauties*, ev'ry where we find.

Sweet Poet, Nature's artless child,
As ever wak'd the soothing strain.
Long may thy pleasing "wood-notes wild,"
Resound along our jocund plain:
And when, with pure poetic flame,
You wake again the sounding lyre,
O! may Ultonia's Genius deign,
Your deathless verses to inspire.

BALLYTRESNA

G.

In 1811, another poem, 'Mary, Flower of the Main' by John Getty, appeared in an American literary publication (*Select Reviews, And Spirit Of The Foreign Magazines*, Philadelphia, 1811), apparently without the author's prior knowledge. An intriguing link with James Orr is possible here, as Orr is also known to have had some of his poems published in America. In any case, John Getty wrote to the *Belfast Monthly Magazine* in 1813 as follows:

To the Proprietors of the Belfast Magazine,

Gentlemen,

The following song appeared in the papers about two years ago, in a very different form; and perhaps I would not have thought any more about it, if I had not been informed lately, that it had been published in an American paper. I own I was a little flattered by the account; but as it contained some expressions that I wished corrected, I have taken the liberty of sending it to you, requesting, if you think it worthy of insertion, a corner of the Belfast Magazine. I confess I would be highly gratified to find they had obtained your approbation.

I remain, Gentlemen,
Your obedient servant,

J. Getty.

Ballytresna, March 15th, 1813

This song by John Getty (bearing some similarity to Orr's 'Song: Written in Winter', and set to the same tune), was published in the *Belfast Monthly Magazine*, April 30, 1813. In fact, the changes from the American version were microscopic.

A SONG.

Tune, "Humours of Glen."

How fresh is the rose in the gay dewy morning.
That peeps with a smile o'er yon eastern hill!
How fair is the lily our gardens adorning!
And fresh is the daisy that blooms by the rill!
But Mary, the rarest, the fairest, sweet flower,
That ever adorn'd the green banks of the Main:
Compared with whose beauty, the eglantine bower,
The rose and the lily, how trifling and vain!

How lovely her bosom, where friendship and feeling
Still heave for misfortune, the dear, tender sigh!
How sweet are her looks ev'ry beauty revealing,
And mild is the lustre that beams in her eye!

The blush of her cheek still outrivals Aurora,
When beauty and music awake the young dawn.
And sweeter her smile than the smile of sweet Flora,
When cowslips and daisies bedeck the gay lawn.

And O! lovely maid! may thy beauties still flourish,
Unnipp'd by the blast of misfortune's rough gale!
May virtue attend thee, thy goodness to nourish,
And no ruffian hand the sweet blossom assail!
May fortune's best smiles, lovely maid, never leave thee,
Through life's fleeting scenes, as thou journey'st along,
And curst be the villain would seek to deceive thee.
Or offer thy virtue and innocence wrong!

Let lordlings exult in their titles and treasure.
Where courts and where grandeur extend their proud blaze;
And proud city beauties may listen with pleasure,
While poets unblushing re-echo their praise;
No more shall they boast of the city or palace,
Bedeck'd with rich beauties, a gay gilded train.
For now there's a fairer adorns our green vallies,
Tis Mary, sweet Mary, the flower of the Main!

In 1818, after the death of Thomson and Orr, another member of the south Antrim Ulster-Scots literary circle, John Dickey of Donegore, published his *Poems on Various Subjects* in Belfast. Instead of the usual alphabetical list of subscribers, Dickey had named them in verse form. Here we discover that 'John Getty of Randlestown' was among the names:

> "John Courtney of Doagh, is no pitiful scrub;
> Two copies are ta'en by Carngranny Book Club.
> John Getty, of Randlestown, listens my strain,
> And Reverend Priest Gribben of Magheralane."

The following year, in 1819, a north Antrim poet, John McKinley of Dunseverick, published his *Poetic Sketches, Descriptive of the Giants Causeway* with 'Mr. John Getty, R.town' among the subscribers.

During the short period of publication of the *Dublin Penny Journal* from 1833 to 1836, John Getty turned from poetry after publishing 'Ballymena's Bonny Jean' in August 1833 and became a regular contributor on a wide range of subjects. These included several short stories or 'narratives' of Ulster-Scots interest, such as 'Old Nannie Boyd—A True Narrative' (*Dublin Penny Journal*, March 29, 1834), and 'The Ghost and the Two Blacksmiths' (*Dublin Penny Journal*, January 17, 1835). But even in his scientific and natural history contributions we find snatches of Ulster-Scots interest. Here are some examples:

1. **'The History and Mode of Curing Butter'**, J.G., Ballymena, *Dublin Penny Journal*, Vol.1, Jan 19, 1833:—[... *Before closing this article, it may he proper to observe, that the manufacture of the famous Dunlop cheese, made in Ayrshire, and said to rival, if not excel, the best English cheese, was first learned in Ireland. A woman, named Barbara Gilmore, came over from Scotland, during the persecution there; and resided some time in Glenwherry, County Antrim, where she learned to manufacture the said cheese, and introduced the mode into the parish of Dunlop, whence it has obtained its name; and it is worthy of remark, that her descendants still reside on the same farm in that parish.*]

2. **'On Lime and Mortar'**, J Getty Ballymena *Dublin Penny Journal*, Vol.1, May 11, 1833:—[... *Lime is found to be heavier after being slacked, and the addi-*

tional weight is owing to part of the water combining with the lime ('slacked' for 'slaked').]

3. **'Combustion'**, J. Getty Ballymena, *Dublin Penny Journal,* Vol 1, July 1833.

4. **'On Comets'**, J Getty Ballymena, *Dublin Penny Journal,* Vol. 2, July 6, 1833.—[*... In the ages of ignorance and superstition, they were regarded as the infallible harbingers of great political and physical convulsions; wars, pestilence, and famine, were among the dreadful evils which they foretold.*]

5. **'On The Death Watch'**, J. Getty Ballymena, *Dublin Penny Journal,* Vol. 2, Aug. 3, 1833.—[*... Still, however, it is a melancholy truth, that too many of the lower ranks of society, and some even of the higher, are but too credulous, even at this day, in believing many of the idle stories which were formerly invented by ignorance and superstition. Amongst these is the belief, which is still retained by many people, in what is vulgarly called the Death Watch. It is an undoubted fact that many people, when waiting upon the sick, hear something resembling the beating of a watch, and which they frequently conclude is sent for a warning before the person's death. Nothing, however, is more certain than that, if they were to observe the same silence at other times, they would hear the beating equally distinct; but at that solemn hour, when we are anxiously waiting on the bed of sickness, we naturally observe the most profound silence; and hence it is, that amidst the stillness of the night, we*

generally hear the Death Watch. … A well known sati-rist sports with the superstitions respecting this insect, in the following lines:

> *"The next insect we call a wood-worm,*
> *That lives in old wood, like a hare in her form;*
> *With teeth or with claws it will bite or will scratch,*
> *And chambermaids christen the worm a death-watch:*
> *Because, like a watch, it always cries click;*
> *Then woe be to those in the house who are sick;*
> *For, as sure as a gun, they will give up the ghost,*
> *If the maggot cries click, when it scratches a post."*
> *SWIFT. Wood an Insect. 1725*

6. **'On the Auroura Borealis'** J.G. Ballymena, in *Dublin Penny Journal*, Vol. 2, August 17, 1833.—[… *The Auroura Borealis, northern lights, or streamers …*]

7. **'Ornithology. On the Different Species of the Lark'**. J. G. Ballymena, County Antrim, *Dublin Penny Journal*, Vol. 2 Dec. 21 1833.—[… *Alanda pralensis, or titlark. … Several have affirmed that it is this bird which follows the cuckoo; hence the common saying, "the cuckoo and the titling." But whether this is the case or not, I cannot positively say. … The snipe, or heather-bleat sings, if singing it can be called, on the wing for many hours. …*]

8. **'Ornithology. On the Swallow and its habits'**, J.G., Ballymena, *Dublin Penny Journal*, Vol. 2 May 1, 1834.

9. **'Moving Bog'**, J. G—y, Ballymena, *Dublin Penny Journal*, Vol 4, Oct. 5 1835.—[*This bog is generally*

known by the name of Slogan, or rather Sluggan bog, and lies on the right of the mail coach road from Randalstown to Ballymena. It is one of the largest in the County of Antrim, measuring upwards of fifteen hundred acres. On Saturday night, September 19th, the inhabitants of the neighbourhood were alarmed by repeated loud reports, in some measure resembling thunder, and which they soon discovered to proceed from the bog. Shortly after the immense mass began to move, and, taking a N.W. direction, spread over about fifty perches of the mail coach road, on which it now lies, from ten to fifteen feet deep. Passing the road, on an inclined plane, it moved on to the river Main, into which it flowed. The water and mud soon formed a channel of about twelve feet deep, in the centre of the part that was moving; and is, at this date, (October 5th,) still running, having nearly dammed up the river Main.]

10. 'The Atropa, or Deadly Night-Shade', J.G. Ballymena, *Dublin Penny Journal*, Vol. 4, May 7. 1836.

As a poet, John Getty was an admiring 'brither bard' to James Orr, the weaver-poet Bard of Ballycarry, and possibly also John Dickey of Donegore. As a schoolmaster-poet he appears to also have had a friendly relationship with Samuel Thomson, the Bard of Carngranny. We have a glimpse of this in Jennifer Orr's scholarly account of Samuel Thomson's correspondence in '*Literary Networks and Dissenting Print Culture in Romantic-Period Ireland*' (2016):—"As Samuel Thomson began his last decline towards death in 1815, he received a friendly letter from John Getty, Ballymena, a fellow schoolmaster poet who had contributed regularly to Union-era journals and newspapers".

But after the death of James Orr and Samuel Thomson in 1816, the schoolmaster-poet John Getty focussed his literary energies on scientific topics. It is tempting, when reading his articles on comets and the aurora borealis in the *Dublin Penny Journal*, to wonder if he, as a boy of about 16, might have come under the influence of Thomson and Orr's former associate, the Rev. James Porter of Greyabbey (who was hanged in 1798). In 1796 and 1797 Porter was travelling the Ulster-Scots countryside to lecture on 'Astronomy, Geography, &c', but reportedly using his 'classes' (and his writings in the *Northern Star*) to organise radical opposition to the government. In any case, John Getty deserves more recognition in his own right as a poet, folk-story collector, educator and scientist. He was deeply rooted in and devoted to his Ulster-Scots community between Ballymena and Randalstown. The rural south Antrim plain of the River Maine that connected these two towns (via Gracehill and Ballytresna) was not only his 'hame kintra', but the 'Genius of the Main' was indeed his inspiration.

The Ghost and the Two Blacksmiths

John Getty

[*This narrative written by John Getty, a schoolmaster of Ballytesna, near Ahoghill, was published in the Dublin Penny Journal, January 17, 1835.*]

Upwards of forty years ago, in the beautiful little Village of Randalstown,

> "*Wham ne'er a town surpasses*
> *For honest men and bonnie lasses,*"
> [Burns – *Tam O'Shanter*]

there lived a blacksmith, named James Walker; he was an industrious, honest man, and regularly attended the Presbyterian house of worship – but still he had his failings. He occasionally took a little too much of the mountain-dew, to quench the spark in his throat, but was accounted a most excellent workman notwithstanding. About a mile and a half from the village, on the road leading to Ahoghill, lived another blacksmith, called Harry Donnell. Harry was in most respects a similar character; for he too had a similar failing, with this exception, that though he had to pass through Randalstown to the chapel, he made it a point never to be seen tipsy on Sunday. At any other time, when he came to the village, James and he were sure to have a drop. During their potations, however, they never meddled with religion, wisely observing, that it was a subject too sacred for discussion over the bottle. Their time was generally employed in discussing the most improved methods of shoeing horses, making spades and plough-irons, &c.; and whatever improvement any of them had made or found out, it was freely imparted to the other.

It happened one year, in the latter part of autumn, that Harry had been detained longer than usual from seeing his friend, – but having got his corn in, and the potatoes secured from the coming frosty blast, he resolved to go to the village to purchase some iron and coals and other articles, but more especially to see his friend, James, and have a glass. He left home in the afternoon of one of the dreary days in November, telling his family not to be uneasy if he should delay longer than usual, being almost certain he would get company home.

As he walked along the road, his eye wandered with delight down the sloping vale of the river Main, where the *then* comfortable farmers resided in independence, and hospitality sat smiling at their board; but, alas! the times are altered there now. He soon reached the town and having made his purchases, and arranged all to his mind, he called at the shop of his friend, James, from whom he received a hearty shake of the hand, with an expression of surprise at his being so long absent.

They immediately went to the sign of the Black Bull, – were shown into the little parlour, where a rousing turf-fire was blazing in the grate, at which they sat down – called for half a pint of spirits, and in a short time a smoking jug of punch was on the table, which they speedily quaffed, discoursing on their usual topics; and the jug was again and again emptied and replenished, till the toll of the curfew informed them it was nine o'clock. Harry then remarked that it was time he was home, adding a wish that he was past Drumarory Bush[1] "where," he said, "so many fearsome

---

[1] Drumarory Bush was a large hawthorn, that grew on the edge of the road, one half mile out of Randalstown in going to Ahoghill, and was

things had been seen, and about which so many alarming stories had been told."

This led them into a discussion on the existence of ghosts, fairies, and other aerial beings: James arguing that there were no such things, and Harry as firmly, maintaining that there were. At last, James, seeing that all his arguments had no effect in convincing Harry, or in removing his fear, proffered to accompany him beyond the dreaded bush; protesting that he feared neither ghost, nor fairy, nor even emissary of the ould boy himself. Harry thankfully accepted his company; and, when matters were thus arranged, they repaired to the bar, to pay the reckoning; after which Harry remarking, that it would be very dangerous to go out in so cold a night after drinking warm punch, without a taste of *raw spirits*, called for another naggin, during the drinking of which their former subject was renewed at the bar, and was attentively listened to by all who surrounded the kitchen fire. At last Harry and James set off; James still protesting that he was as little afraid of passing Drumarory bush as any other bush.

Their discourse ran mostly on the, same subject till,

"*The dreaded bush was drawing nigh,*
"*Whar ghosts and witches nightly cry;*"

but, to their great inward satisfaction, all was quiet.

Scarcely had they proceeded a few paces further, when a blazing light sprung up and seemed to dance about the bush with great rapidity; this put them to a stand. James said, "In God's name we'll

---

famous in country story, as the haunt of fairies, witches, and evil spirits; and even the devil himself was said to "be seen at it"; so that it was a place very few liked to pass at a late hour. In fact, the writer, when a boy, durst not pass it alone after night-fall. It is now cut down, so that its place is no more to be found; but a little above where it stood is a rise in the road, still called Drumarory Brae.

see what it is;" but they had not gone more than a few steps when something clad in white stepped on the road, giving a wild unearthly scream; and just opposite to them they heard another still more terrific. James's philosophy instantly forsook him; and both took to their heels back to the town; but still, as they ventured to peep round, they saw the white ghost, and the light following, till they came opposite Feehoge, where the apparition and light glided down a dark avenue, and disappeared. Over-exertion and terror made them now slacken their pace; but they soon renewed it, on hearing a foot coming fast behind them; they stopped, however, on hearing a human voice cry out, "If you are Christians or men, I entreat you to stand, for I am frightened out of my senses by a ghost." This person soon joined them; and, to their great joy, they found it was Jamie Irons, the barber of Randalstown, who declared he would faint, or perhaps die, unless he would soon get a glass of whiskey. This he was promised, as they were now at the head of the town. They came to the same inn, called for a pint of spirits, of which Jamie got a large share, and related to the amazed inmates their strange adventure – Irons confirming it by declaring, that as he was coming up Feehoge avenue, a white woman or ghost, followed by a blazing light, passed him, and afterwards glided, without any noise, through the orchard-hedge.

The whiskey soon restored their wasted spirits; and Jamie seeing no chance of any more liquor coming in, began to remark that it would be a pity Harry should be detained in town all night. That as there were now three of them, he proposed they should go to Drumarory, and see Harry past; offering himself as a *vidette*. To this they agreed; and, taking another glass, they set off; Irons, as he promised, being some perches in advance. They soon arrived at the bush – but nothing was to be seen or heard, save the distant swells and falls of the river Main: so leaving Harry on the top of Drumarory Brae, the two returned to town. Harry being now in full spirits, and, as he thought, out of all danger, began to grow quite courageous – swearing that he could beat any fellow who durst oppose him on the road – nor was he afraid of the very Old Boy. The whiskey was now taking full effect. In this way he went on till he reached Seymour's-bridge, a mile out of town, where there was, and still ought to be, a school-house; against the gable of which he leaned himself, in order to rest; when, looking towards the west, across the road, he saw on the height opposite, a man, in the attitude of challenging him to fight! Harry instantly stepped on the road, ordered him to come down, and keep less vapouring, or he would soon make him repent it; to this the man seemed to pay no attention, but still kept taunting him as formerly. At this, Harry losing all patience, made a race at him; but forgetting there was an old gravel-pit, generally full of water, on a level with the road, and directly opposite, he plunged into it over head and ears, and would probably have been drowned had he not been providentially rescued by a young man coming down the road at the time, who heard the plunge. When brought out, he could hardly be persuaded that what he took for a man in the attitude of fighting was nothing but a large *rag-wort* waving in the wind. He, however, resolved, in future, never to be drunk after night in Randalstown, or stay there late, which resolution he faithfully kept till the day of his death.

The story of the ghost and the two smiths passed current in the town and country; and was firmly believed by almost every one; and there are still some people living in that neighbourhood, who would yet vouch for its authenticity; but the truth is, Jamie Irons, as he informed the writer, was the ghost himself: he was, perhaps, the greatest man for tricks of this sort, ever bred in the county of Antrim; and, though his countenance was indicative of nothing but wisdom, and the utmost gravity, so that he was seldom seen to smile, yet he was of a most playful and merry dis-position, and delighted in humbugging every one that he knew was self-conceited or too opinionative. On the night mentioned, he was sitting at the inn's kitchen fire; and, when James Walker so frequently protested that he feared no ghost or evil spirit, he resolved to put his courage to a fair trial. Getting, therefore, a white sheet, a keenoge,[2] and a bunch of splinters of bog-fir, such as is used by fishers at night, he proceeded before the two smiths to Drumarory; and, with the assistance of a person he brought for the purpose, performed, as can be easily imagined, the above deception on the blacksmiths.

J. G. [John Getty]
Ballymena.

---

[2] *Keenoge* or *Cunea,* is a turf-coal, rolled tightly in tow or flax, so that you may carry it a long way in your pocket without its kindling; but when opened out to the air, it instantly becomes, as it were, alive again, and will kindle any combustible.

Old Nannie Boyd — A True Narrative [of Slemish and the Braid in the aftermath of 1798]

Philip Robinson

[*This narrative, containing much Ulster-Scots dialogue, was written by John Getty, a schoolmaster from Ballytrasna near Ahoghill, and published in the Dublin Penny Journal March 29, 1834, with the following note: "It affords us great pleasure to comply with the request of a respected correspondent, by inserting the foregoing simple narrative of facts; alike honorable to the character of the officer and the humble individual to whom it refers; and may serve as a set off to some of those tales of cruelty and revenge which, in describing the peasantry of some other portions of our country, we are, in candour, compelled to insert in our journal. — Ed."*]

One evening, during the severe winter of 1799, as Nannie Boyd[1] came in from the bhyre (cow-house), with a pail of milk in her hand, she thus addressed her family —

"This is gaun to be a very severe night, childer. I saw in the morning that the tap o' Slieve Bawn, between us and the glens, was white

---

[1] It is customary in some parts of Ireland, and in Scotland, to call a married woman by her maiden name: Nannie's husband, who was some time dead, was Thomas Crawford.

wi' sna'; and I doubted a' day we would have a fa': I hae been now upwards of forty years living in this place, and I dinna remember to hae seen a mair gloomy and dismal-looking evening. Gang you, Bab, and put the sheep in some safe and sheltry place: they are a' come down frae Knockrammer, as if led by some natural fore-boding, to Knockcoghram, on purpose, it would seem, to be near the houses and human aid: and gang you, Jack, and bring in mair peats; for you may depend it will be an easier task now than in the morning: and, Jean, said she to the girl, bring in plenty o' water."

Her orders no one disputed. Her son, wrapping himself up in his great coat, set off with the dog to the hill. The turf and water were soon brought in; and a large fire put on. Nannie took her seat at her wheel in the corner; and several of the neighbours' girls, who had, as was the custom, come in with their wheels, formed a semi-circle round the fire, and commenced their nightly task with one of Burns's songs —

"The gloomy night is gathering fast."

An hour had elapsed, when Nannie stopped her wheel, and said —

"I wonder what detains Bab sae lang on the hill?"

"Hoot," said one of the girls, "do ye think that Bab will be on Knockcoghram, and no gang owre to the Brownstown, and see his sweet-heart."

Nannie seemed satisfied, and resumed her wheel. The wind had now risen, and a choking drift was falling fast. A rap came to the door; but as every one lifted the latch, and came in without any ceremony, little attention was paid to it; till a second was given, when one of the girls rose, and opened the door. A man of genteel appearance entered, covered with snow, from which being disengaged, he thus addressed the family:

"This is a very snowy night, and I believe I have nearly lost my

way. Is there any person in this house that will conduct me safe
to Broughshane, and I will reward him handsomely."

"I'm thinking," said Nannie, "ye had better come forward to
the fire, an' warm yersel'; its an unco cauld night and I doubt
there's nane in the town could gang wi' ye, but my son, Bab; and
he's no in at present. Sit down at the fire, and we'll see what can
be done."

The stranger took a seat; and Nannie, without saying another
word, lighted a candle, stepped into the room, and soon returned
with a plate of butter, some oat-cakes, and the heel of a cheese,
which she placed on the kitchen-table; saying to the stranger —

"Turn round your chair, and take a bite o' bread; ye hae, maybe,
travelled a lang road the day, and ye canna be the worse o' eating
something."

The gentleman thanked her, turned round, and took a hearty
luncheon; adding, "that he had come from Cushendall, by what
the people there told him was the shortest way to Broughshane;
though I suspect," said he, "that they intended to put me wrong;
yet, I must acknowledge, that they told me also, that the road I
was travelling on, would take me to my destination."

"Might I mak sae free," said Nannie, "as to ask what business
ye follow, that obliged ye to come owre the hills at this season o'
the year. It was weel the ground was frozen; otherwise ye might
hae been lost a' thegither."

"Indeed, Madam," said the stranger, "I am a soldier: at present
under strict orders to join my regiment, now in Ballymena;" giving
his name at the same time.

At mention of the word soldier, one of the girls slipped out.

"And if ye be a soldier," said Nannie, "why but ye hae on a
red coat? I ay like to see folk appearing in their proper colours."

"That is very right," said the gentleman; "but I only arrived
from Scotland yesterday; and as the people in this country were
so lately in a state of insurrection, I thought it safest to put on

coloured clothes, lest I might meet with some insult, or, perhaps worse, from the inhabitants, among whom I am a total stranger."

"Ye needna hae been sae scar'd," replied Nannie; "for ye woudna hae met wi' ony thing but civility either in the glens, or in the braid; that is, provided ye conducted yeresel' discreetly, as a stranger ought to do; for though the glens folk are maistly Roman Catholics, and we in the Braid, maistly Presbyterians, yet we live on the best terms. When ony o' our folk gangs down there, they are treated wi' the utmost kindness and friendly feeling; and when they come up here, we do what we can to mak a return."

"I wish, Madam," answered the stranger, "that this was the universal practice in Ireland: but I forget Broughshane, which, if possible, I must be in to-night."

"Indeed," answered Nannie, "I just think ye may be thankfu' that ye're in bigged wa's. Do ye hear how awfu' the storm is raging without, an' the drift whirling through the air; (I wish Bab was hame); look at that window and see how its blinded wi' the sna'. Ye man e'en content yeresel' whar ye are till the morning; — I can gie' ye a clean bed, and plenty o' blankets, which ye'll find usefu' on sae cauld a night."

The gentleman went to the door, looked out, and returned; saying, "he would be happy to accept of her friendly offer, as the night was getting still worse." Shortly after, her son, Bob, returned, almost choked with drift, and covered with snow; from which being disengaged, he sat down at the fire, saying that he never experienced so severe a night.

"This is a stranger;" said his mother, "that wants somebody to conduct him to Broughshane; but I think he is better here than out in sic a night; he's a military man, and gaun on some important business I suppose; but naebody could gang out the night on ony account."

"It would be," replied her son, "a tempting o' Providence to gang the length o' Skirry, through sic storm, he will, I hope, content himself whar he is till the marning."

The stranger and Bob soon got into conversation; the former related many interesting anecdotes in military life; and described many of the towns in which he had been quartered; and some of the most remarkable highland hills, glens, and mountains that he had visited; and with which he seemed quite familiar; but when he told them that the city of London contained more inhabitants than the counties of Antrim and Down put together, they were amazed, and scarcely gave credit to his assertion. — Bob, on the other hand, told him that the place where he now was, was called the Fourtowns of Skirry in the braid; that though it was a mountainous district, the inhabitants were a tolerably well informed class, having a respectable book-club; and the newspapers circulating regularly among them, &c.

In this way the night passed till bed time; and after all the night's avocations were finished, Bob brought forward the "Bigha bible, ance his father's pride" and seating himself, said, with becoming gravity, "let us worship God;" — choosing a psalm, he commenced singing, in which he was joined by the stranger, and all the family; and afterwards he read a chapter in the bible, and then knelt down to pray, offering up the thanks of a grateful and pious heart to the dispenser of all good, for the protection which his humble roof afforded them in such a dreadful night; imploring His protecting care over such as were so unfortunate as to be overtaken by the storm, or perhaps, perishing in the snow.

The gentleman, after all was finished, remarked that he almost fancied himself at home in Scotland; observing at the same time, that from the accounts which he had been taught to believe, he did not suppose that any portion of the inhabitants of Ireland were so strictly religious; but he was assured by Bob that what he now witnessed was a common practice in many districts of Ireland.

The night still continued wild, while the tempest o'er the chimney top, sounded a melancholy dirge. They all repaired to rest, but Jack still thought on —

> *"Ilk happing bird, wee helpless thing,*
> *That in the merry months o' spring*
> *Delighted me to hear thee sing;*
> > *What comes o' thee?*
> *Whare wilt thou cow'r thy chittering wing,*
> > *And close thy e'e?"* [Burns, 'A Winter's Night']

It is enough to say, that the next morning was as bad as the preceding night; and the storm continued with unabated fury till the following morning, during which time the stranger amused himself reading the newspaper, and some of the books belonging to the club; and after the weather became settled, it was deemed impracticable to go any length from the house.

> *"Since path is none, save that to bring*
> *The needful water from the spring."*
> [Walter Scott, *Marmion*, Canto V]

But in a few days the road was deemed passable; and he, after proffering Nannie a handsome remuneration for her trouble, which she peremptorily refused, proceeded under the guidance of Bob, to the road leading to Broughshane, which, after much difficulty, they gained. Here the gentleman again requested Bob to accept of some recompence for his trouble, but this he absolutely refused; and after a cordial shake hands, and many thanks on the part of the stranger, they parted.

It is generally known that the leaders of the insurgents in the county of Antrim, in case they were defeated, had appointed the mountain of Slemish,[2] a high, and conspicuous hill, near the

---

[2] The two hills, Skirry and Slemish, (the latter of which is sometimes spelt Sleive Mis or Slieve Mois,) mentioned above. The former is a

centre of the county of Antrim, as their chief place of rendezvous; and at this place they were to consult what was next to be done. It happened that a Mr. A. H——y, who had the command of the pikemen, or at least a party of them, at the battle of Antrim, was wounded by a musket-ball in the front of his shoulder, which penetrated so far, that it had to be extracted from the opposite side; with difficulty and peril, he made his way to Slemish; and through some means or other, got shelter, though a perfect stranger, in Nannie Boyd's till his wound would be whole, which it was at the time of the stranger's calling, though he was still unable to use it. Mr. A. H——y happened to be in a neighbour's house, the night already mentioned; and the girl hearing the stranger say that he belonged to the military, she conjectured he was a spy; and so she warned Mr. A. H——y, not to venture into the house till the stranger had left the place, in consequence of which he remained where he was till the gentleman's departure. At this period orders had been issued by the military, who then had the

---

green rocky hill of easy ascent, and has on its top an old church, said to be founded by St. Patrick; and on a stone near it is a hollow, in some respects resembling the impression of a foot, which is said to be that of St. Patrick himself, when he, one day, stepped from Slemish to Skirry — the distance being only about two miles. There is a burying ground at the old church, exclusively for Roman Catholics; and in the ruins of an old vault or tomb, a branch of the O'Neill family still deposit their dead. It was at Skirry and not Slemish, that tradition says St. Patrick kept the flock of Milco. Slemish lies southward of Skirry, on the mearing between Glenwherry parish and that of the Braid — A writer in a contemporary publication says Slemish is composed of *greenstone*: I do not know what he exactly means by that term; but one thing I am sure of, is, that it is composed of basalt, and of the Floetz Trap formation, and is about 1390 feet above the level of the sea.

administration of the law, that a paper containing the names of all the family, males and females, should be posted on the outside door of every inhabited house. This was done on Nannie Boyd's; but the stranger either did not, or seemed not, to take any notice of it. He well knew, however, that all the family were not at home; for Nannie had informed him that she had two other sons, who were tradesmen, and would not be home for some time.

During the summer of that year, one night, when all the family was fast asleep, old Nannie was awakened by the trampling of feet about the house, and a loud and furious knocking at the door, demanding entrance. She rose hastily, and lighted a candle; when she found, to her great dismay, that the whole house was surrounded by a large party of military, foot and horse: she opened the door, (in great trepidation,) as was demanded; and an officer, accompanied by a number of soldiers, entered; but the moment the officer saw her, he ordered the men to retire; and stretching out both his hands to her, asked her how she was?

She drew back, saying, "that she didna think he would hae been sae unkind as to come about her house at that hour o' the night, wi' a parcel of soldiers to frighten her sae; nor did she think she had deserved sic treatment at his hand."

He clasped both her hands, while a tear started in his eye. "No, my good woman, do not think me so base; I knew nothing of the place I was coming to, being conducted by an informer, who told the commanding officer in Ballymena, that he would, for a certain sum, bring us to a house in which was one of the rebel leaders; but it is, perhaps, best, that I was appointed to command the party." So saying, he stepped out, and ordered the men to keep their stations round the house, and let no one escape; adding, that he was acquainted with the people of the house, and would search it himself; which he did very strictly; but there was *one place* that he did not come near, and there lay concealed poor Mr. A. H——y, in trembling expectation of his fate. Finding none but the family, he ordered the men away; and with a hearty shake hands, and warm and fervent prayer from old Nannie for his welfare, he took his leave. Long after the officer left the country, Mr. A. H——y was made a prisoner, and lodged in Carrickfergus gaol; but as no witness appeared against him, he was at length liberated; when he went to Glasgow, and died there only a few years ago. Some years after her son's marriage, Nannie went to reside with her daughter at Raloo, where she died; and is buried in Raloo graveyard, near Larne. Her son, Bob, emigrated to America, and died in 1832. Many years after, when Jack had, by his industry, advanced himself to a higher grade in society, he happened to spend an evening among a number of literary characters and other gentlemen in Belfast; one of whom related, by way of anecdote, some of the principal events above mentioned; Jack viewed him more minutely, and discovered that he was the same person who had lodged with Nannie during the snow storm; and on making himself known, and reminding him of some minute circumstances, it is impossible to describe the kindness and friendship which he experienced from the officer, whose enquiries about Nannie and her family were sincere and affectionate.

J. G. [John Getty]

'Tha Boat Sang' (translation) by St. Columbanus, c. 600 AD

THA BOAT SANG

Oor keel, hagged oot o forest timmer,
Swep doon tha twa-hoarn't Rhine.
Wrocht ticht thegither an weel caulkit tae
Noo she floats on tha apen watter.
Wha-hae, ye boy ye!
Lang may tha echas soon,
wi oor 'Wha-hae'!

A wile wun brays, whup't up oot o naewhar.
Doon tha whammlin torrent teems.
Ay, we hae strenth eneuch, but, us men,
Tae gar tha stoarm be queeit.
Wha-hae, ye boy ye!
Lang may tha echas soon,
wi oor 'Wha-hae'!

Ettle on, wi aefauld hairt, an niver let up.
Push on fair forrit. Keep her straicht an true.
Luk see, tha thunner cloods skail, tha wun draps;
A nivir-fleggin hairt o zeal bates aa.
Wha-hae, ye boy ye!
Lang may tha echas soon,
wi oor 'Wha-hae'!

Thole it, boys, an keep yersels strang.
Far waur nor this ye hae bin throu.
Thole on, tha en's in sicht,
An better things is yit tae cum.
Wha-hae, ye boy ye!
Lang may tha echas soon,
wi oor 'Wha-hae'!

Sae, whan thon hatesome fae, oor hairts atteck
Hoakin in tha deepmaist pairts tae tempt oor sowl.
Sing yer hairts oot, boys,
Hae mind o Christ,
An crie, 'Wha-hae'!

Hairts o steel, scoarn Satan's sleekit wyes
Airm'd fur tha fecht, wi tha micht o richt.
Sing yer hairts oot, boys,
Hae mind o Christ,
An crie, 'Wha-hae'!

Strang faith, wi halie zeal, bates aa.
Tha oul divil, noo pit doon, haes aa his erras brok.
Sing yer hairts oot, boys,
Hae mind o Christ,
An crie, 'Wha-hae'!

St. Colombanus (543-615):
The first 'Scotch-Irish' Laggan Poet?

Philip Robinson

St. Columbanus sailed from near Bangor Abbey with about a
dozen other *Scotti Hibernicus* (Scotch-Irish) monks from Bangor

about the year 590 AD. After many years of mission across France, Switzerland and Northern Italy, he died in 615 – at the Abbey he founded in Bobbio, Italy, after boating up the Rhine and traversing the Alpine lakes. He wrote several poems in Latin, the best known being 'Carmen Navale' (The Boat Song), circa 600 AD.

Could the *Scotti-Hibernicus* Columbanus have been the first documented poet from the Laggan, over 1000 years before William Starrat was publishing his Laggan Scotch poems between 1719 and 1753?

Almost all we know of Columbanus was written by the monk Jonas of Bobbio shortly after his death in 615. This *VITAE SANC-TORUM COLUMBANI* (Life of St. Columbanus) tells us that he was of the nation of the Scots that lived in Ireland, and was born in a place called by the inhabitants 'Lagen' (*in Lagenorum finibus natus*):

> "*Columbano duce vel Columba duodecim monachi natione Scotti, quae gens non tam legibus quam fidei christianae fervore reliquas tunc longe praestabat, viri admodum provectae aetatis ex Hibernia profecti ad Britanniam Gallicam appulerunt, ibique paulisper remorati, tandem Gallias adire constituerunt ad mores hominum inquirendos, ut si ingenia repperissent ad salutem recipiendam habilia, ibidem consisterent, sin aliter, ad vicinas nationes transirent. Erat autem Columbanus in Lagenorum finibus natus, liberalibus litteris a pueritia usque ad virilem aetatem institutus ....*"

[Columban, who is also called Columba... was born on the island of Ireland.... Here lives the race of the Scots, who, although they lack the laws of the other nations, flourish in the doctrine of Christian strength, and exceed in faith all the neighbouring tribes. Columban was born amid the beginnings of that race's faith. ... When he left his birthplace, called by the inhabitants, Lagen-land, he betook himself to a holy man named Sinell, who at this time was distinguished among his countrymen for his unusual piety and knowledge of the Holy Scriptures ...]

According to Jonas of Bobbio, Columbanus left his 'Lagen' home when a still a youth by stepping over his mother's prostrate body in the doorway of their home, as she begged him not to leave. He fled to Cleenish Island near Enniskillen on Lough Erne, where St. Sinell began instructing him in the Scriptures (apparently becoming particularly learned on the Psalms). He then moved to Bangor Abbey in the late 6th century, where he adopted their peculiar practice of 'Perpetual Praise'. This involved a rota of monks singing their way through the entire Books of 150 Psalms every week.

The recent identification of Columbanus's birth-place of the 'Lagen' with somewhere in Leinster (or even in west Cork) is entirely speculative – "*Lagáin*" in Gaelic simply means 'low lying district' – and the place-name occurs throughout Ireland. But the Donegal 'Laggan' is not only the best-known, but also the most probable birth-place of Columbanus, given that his runaway destination as a youth from his home was not Bangor Abbey, but Cleenish Island in Fermanagh.

Thegither An Apairt

Fiona McDonald

She had nae mine o it –
Whut tuk her thonner
Jaist afore dayligan, in Septemmer.
Tha oul blak yetts scraik't
Eneuch tae wak tha deid.
She fun thaim – Wullie an Maggie –
Doon tha side o tha Meetin Hoose,
Wi blak granite mairkit,
A geranium in a clie pot
Frae some cuzzin.
The'd cum in frae tha toonlanns
Iverie sennicht,
Wi tha maist o thair freens an neibors –
Quhile toonfowks gaed tha ither wie,
Tae Echt Mile Brig.

1 March 2005

Rathfrilan Fair

Fiona McDonald

Aroon a hunnèr yeir syne, in tha Sooth o Coontie Doon,
Leeved a boy by tha name o Truesdale, near oul Rathfrilan toon.
His mither caa'd him Francis, bot maist fowks gied him Frank.
He wus a boul big hallion, bot he'd siller in tha bank.

Weel, Frank he wusnae merriet, an he had a fairm o lan.
He wusnae mair nor fiftie, and life wus quare an gran.
Fur he cud dae whutiver he plaised, wi deil tha wife tae barge,
An monie a yin wushed he wus Frank, no lannit wi some oul
    targe.

Ae Fair Day moarn, Frank hitcht tha trep an set aff fur tha toon,
Frae tha fairm at Ballynagappog, strecht up tha hill an roon,
Tae tha Kirk Square whar he pued up, ayont an oul stane barn,
Whar he spied twathie cronies, stannin fur a smoke an haein a
    yarn.

"Ach Billie Rab!" quo Frank wi glee, "whar hae ye bin, oul freen?
An whut aboot ye, Joey? An hoo's tha wife an wean?"
Oul Frank he wus in quare guid foarm, as he pit tha meer awa,
Bot he seen she had a feed o coarn an a guid wee bed o straa.

Noo tha boys wus feelin drouthie, wi aa tha crack o tha Fair,
Sae Frank bocht thaim baith a whuskey, an the' bocht a clattèr
    mair.
Afore lang the' wur richtlie, an liltin sangs o yore,
Tha mair the' cudnae houl a tune – ye cud tell the' wur hauf tore.

Tha lanlaird o tha yillhoose, telt thaim, "Na. Nae mair!
Fur youse is pittin dacent fowk aff cummin in tha dure."
Wee Joe wus oxter-cogglet oot, an telt no tae luk doon,
On accoont o whan he daen it, tha flair wus birlin roon.

Puir Rab near boaked his ring up whan the' got oot in tha air,
Sae tha boys aa thocht the'd gang aff hame, afore thar day got
          waur.
Frank gaed tae get tha oul grey meer, By Sowl, bot no too quick,
Fur tha mair yin fit gaed forrits, tha ither stauchert bak.

Wi Meggie got atween tha trams (A dinnae mine jaist hoo)
An collar, haims an harnish on, Frank cried oot, "A'm aff, noo".
He sprachlet up intae tha sate, an it wus a sicht tae see,
Fur whar yin meer stud fower oor bak, afore him noo wus three!

Noo, Rathfrilan bes a ticht wee toon, bigged on a hill, at tha
          croon.
An nae matter whut wie in ye lan, ye'll hae a stye raa doon.
Sae whan he set aff hameairt bun, Frank tuk it gye an cannie,
Til John Barleycorn cheepit in his lug, "Ye'r drivin lake ma gran-
          nie."

Sae, wi spairks fleein frae tha wheels, an tha pechin o tha pownie,
It wusnae lang tae Frank cried, "Hup", as he spied his ain fairm
          loanie.
Bot tha reins wus like twa washin lines, an he niver hit tha brak,
Sae Frankie an tha pownie, that tuk tha turn ower quick.

Tha trep it coupt clean ower, an Frank wus kilt stane deid.
A ledge he niver felt a thing, fur he landit on his heid.
T'wus brither Tam wha fun him, liein fornenst tha sheuch,
Wi fanklit airms an broo stove in, boys, he wus lukkin ruch.

Tha sistèrs baa'ed an greetit, fur the' wur affleectit sair,
The' wur pooerfu fan o brither Frank, an vext he wus nae mair.
Tha freens an neebours cam tae moarn, an gie thair simpathie
An aa ye hearit wus, "Boys a Dear", or "Och Anee, Anee".

. . . .

Frank's liein in a kirkyaird noo, weel plantit six fit unnèr
An gin ye tak strang drink an drive ye'll mebbe join him thonner
Sae whan ye'r gan oot on tha toon, lea tha motthor weel alane
An gin ye cannae get a taxi, jaist ye dannèr hame yer lane.

29 July 2005

May Crommelin compares some 'Scotch' words to Frisian

[**Editor's note:** In this 1884 extract from *A Visit in a Dutch Country House*, by May Crommelin of Carrowdore, the Ulster authoress of *Orange Lily* and other books compares some 'Scotch' and Frisian words with her Dutch host on a visit to the Netherlands.]

… The children were brought in to be admired by their neighbors and relations. … One four-year-old lovely cherub, Schelto, was coaxed on his father's knee to recite some baby poetry learnt as a greeting for his grandmother's birthday. This, beginning in a murmur, listened to with deep interest, ended in a triumphant shout amid loud applause. …

"There is a Scotch name just the same as that of my boy, Schelto, I have been told?" said the Baron inquiringly. But as "Sch" is pronounced in Dutch something between a rasping choke and a cough – first, *Sh*, and then a horrible sound as if a fishbone had stuck in one's throat (Oh, the torture of trying to pronounce Scheveningen rightly!), I was puzzled a little before suggesting Sholto. "That is it – all right! It is a Friesland name, and Friese and Scotch have many words all the same."

"Why, of course. I will tell you a common rhyme we have," put in Hugo –

"Bread, butter, and cheese,
Is good English, and good Friese."

"And your Dutch *Kom binnen* (Come in), always reminds me of the 'Come ben' of a Scotch peasant wife," I added, in contribution to our philological efforts, further discerning that the house stood by the *beek* of Leyden, answering to our beck, save that it is a sluggish stream indeed; while the Friesland terms *binnen* and *buiten* for inside and outside the house, might be the "but and ben" of Scottish inner and outer rooms.

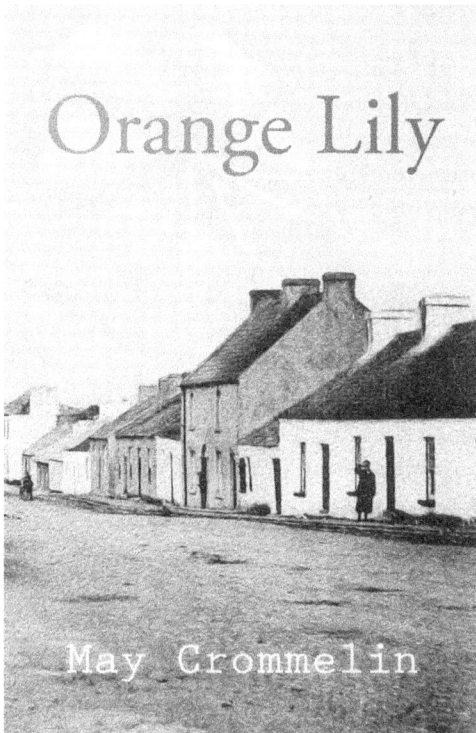

Milwaukee

Philip Robinson

[**Editor's note:** The following poem was written by Philip Robinson at the request of Jim Shannon MP for a poem suitable for reading at an event in Milwaukee a couple of years ago. Not surprisingly, there was nothing in the existing Ulster-Scots literature, so nothing daunted Philip penned this poem, tongue firmly in cheek!]

Yin nicht oor picture-hoose was thrang.
Ma sowl, it was a 'talkie'.
Ye wudnae credit it ava,
It was aboot Milwaukee.

The mair it was in black an white,
James Stewart was but a laddie,
We aa thocht he was ower ocht,
A cooboy – an a baddie.

For Jamie Stewart, we knowed richt weel,
The mair o his big hat.
Was ayeways gye an prood tae be
Scotch-Irish, for aa o that.

Noo here A stan, frae Greba toon,
Up tae ma oxters sweetin,
Anither Jamie prood tae be,
Amang yis at this meetin.

Sae, tak guid heed o aa ye hear,
An eat what's pit afore ye.
It michtnae be a guid while tae,
Ye're bak in oul Milwaukee.

Huevie an tha Pownie

Paittie McIlboy, Greba

Foartie-five year bak, ma Da bocht me this wee gray pownie for Chrisamas, a powerfu pet o a thing, an wile quate. Misty cud even apen tha back dorr an redd tha kitchin table if ma Ma hadnae tha grub pit awa an it wus jaist left oot.

At thon time, naebodie went tae dae tha shappin. Tha shappin cum til ye, in an oul rid van. Huevie had been cummin tae tha Hill fur years. He stairtit wi ma Grannie an cum iverie Friday nicht tae he quat wark aathegither. He wus a wee man, licht built, an he wus aye weerin an oul broon shap coat an a flet kep.

Noo Heuvie liked a drink, an at Christmas time he wud aye be gien a trait at maist o tha cals he made. Tha Hill wus his last stap on a Friday nicht an tha ootcum wus that he wus fu o tha Chrisamas spurit whun he landed, an bi tha time he got his supper an twarthie mair drinks frae ma Da, he wus weel oil't. Noo a funny thing aboot Heuvie wus that as he got a drink or twa, tha kep wus twustit roon a bit on his heid, an bi tha time he left ma Da it wus on sidewyes.

There wus nae breathalysers then an monies a time we wunnered hoo Heuvie iver made it hame tae Newton. But this Friday wus a gye frostie moonlicht nicht an tha loanen at that time run thru twa fiels tae tha road. That meant thrie gates tae apen an shut behin ye. Whun Heuvie got tae tha seycant gate, tha coul air had got tae him an he needit tae mak his wattèr. There wus a wee bit o snaw on tha grun an Heuvie stairted tae mak his mairk, but he didnae see Misty agin tha snaw an tha furst thing he felt wus this big wat tongue rinnin up tha side o his jaa.

Noo needless tae say Heuvie didnae shut tha gate behin him.

He went hame wat an stane coul sober tae Newton, an efter that he aye stayed in the lichts o tha van whun he apen't an shut tha gate. But tha nixt Friday he had fun his sense o humour agane an tuk great delicht in tellin tha yairn agin himsel.

A Wee Danner

Paittie McIlboy, Greba

"C'mon boy, get oot o yer bed, we haetae tak tha kye tae tha Islans."
Ma Da stairtit monies a Setterday moarnin wi this shout, bot somewye ye didnae mine.

Shair eneuch, ye had a thrie mile waak aheid o ye, mebbe far mair, fur ye had tae rin aheid o tha coos an calfs an stan in a slap or loanin en, an then whun the' wur aa bye, ye had tae rin like tha divil himsel, tae get bye them afore the' got tae tha nixt slap.

It wusnae sae bad if it wus only tha kye an tha aul bull by thirsels. Tha auld yins knowed whar the' wur gan; an the' maun hae liked it doon thonner as much as we did, fur the' wud jist danner efter ma da at thair leisure, an if the' did happen tae luk doon a loanin en, ma da jist shoutit *"c'mon c'mon"*, an the' startit efter him agane, sae we hadnae sae much rinnin tae dae. At yin time we had an auld whiteheid bull, an whun he wus gan wi us , it wus even better, fur he wus gye slow at tha waakin an wus aye at tha bak, sae we used tae throw oor leg ivver his bak an get a ride, as weel as a rest, an ye know whun A think on it, he niver even alter't his step.

In very wairm wather, rinnin efter tha wee calfs made ye quare an thirsty an boys did ye luk forrit tae getting a drink o coul watter frae tha wee wal aboot half wye doon tha estate waa. But ye only had time fur twa or thrie moothfaas supped oot o yer cupped han, an then ye had tae rin again. Tha best watter, aa tha same, wus at tha en o tha waak, oot o tha wal on tha Mid Isle. Ye got time tae hae a dacent drink here, a big tin mugfu liftit oot o a white enamel bucket. Ye'll niver buy watter fae onywhar tae bate tha taste o thon.

Yince tha kye wur ontae tha Islan, an ye had got yer drink o watter, ye cum tae tha best bit o aa. Ma Da's Aunt Alice leeved in tha wee hoose on Mid Islan, an whun she saw ye cumin ivver tha roan, (that wus tha stane pad ivver tae tha Islan), she wud a had tha tay on tha table bi tha time ye wur there. Even wi'oot electric tha tay wus quicker here nor at hame, fur tha big kettle wus ayewyes singin on tha range, an wus pit on agane as soon as tha tay wus wat.

Tha smell o that wee hoose wus something else, wi fresh baked sodas an wheatens an hame made butter an jam, it still makes ma teeth watter. A can see tha Swan print on tha patt o butter, an ma Da an Aunt Alice an Jack sittin haein a yairn an takin tha tay jist as if it happened yisterday, bot ye know that wus near on fiftie yeir ago.

19/5/07

The Wet Wooing

A Narrative of Ninety-Eight

Samuel Ferguson

[**Editor's note:** This short Ulster-Scots 'kailyard' novel is set in 1798, in the Antrim hills near Glenwhirry where the Gilliland family farm of Sir Samuel Ferguson's mother was located. While the narrative is in English, the Ulster-Scots dialogue of the local characters is presented with unique accuracy for such an early piece. The novel, which was published in *Blackwood's Edinburgh Magazine* in 1832, also contains one of Ferguson's Ulster-Scots poems ("The Canny Courtship") within the text.]

It was in the autumn of 1798, when the North of Ireland had settled down into comparative tranquillity, that I took up my quarters at Knowehead, the grazing farm of a substantial relative, in the remote pastoral valley of Glen—[1]

The second morning of my stay, I had fished a considerable distance up the river; but having broken my top in an unlucky leap, was sitting in impatient bustle, lapping the fracture, and lamenting my ill fortune, as ever and anon I would raise my eyes and see the fresh curl running past my feet; when I perceived by the sudden blackening of the water, and by an ominous but indescribable sensation of the air, that something unusual was brewing overhead. I looked up: there it was, a cloud, low-hung and lurid, and stretching across the whole northern side of the horizon. I

---

[1] Glenwhirry near Broughshane, east of Ballymena in Co. Antrim, was the home of Samuel Ferguson's mother's family.

had scarce time to gather my clews and bobbins into a hurried wisp, and take shelter under an overhanging bank hard by, when down it came, heavy, hissing, and pelting the whole surface of the river into spray. I drew myself close to the back of the hollow, where I lay in a congratulatory sort of reverie, watching the veins of muddy red, as they slowly at first, and then impetuously flowed through, and finally displaced the dark spring water – the efforts of the beaten rushes and waterflags, as they quivered and flapped about under the shower's battery – the gradual increase of swell and turbulence in the river opposite; and lower down, the war which was already tossing and raging at the conflux, where

> *"Tumbling brown, the burn came down,*
> *And roar'd frae bank to brae."*

But why do I dilate upon an aspect thus wild and desolate, when I could so much more pleasantly employ my reader's and my own mind's eye with that which next presented itself? I confess, so pleasant was the contrast then, that I still, in recalling that scene to memory, prepare myself, by the renewed vision of its dreariness and desolation, for the more grateful reception of an image than which earth contains none lovelier – it was a lovely girl. She fled thither for shelter: I did not see her until she was close by me; but never surely did man's eyes rest on a fairer apparition. I have, at this instant, every lineament of the startled beauty, as, drawing back with a suppressed cry and gesture of alarm, she shrank from the unexpected companion who stood by her side; for I had started from my reverie, and now presented myself, baring my head in the rain with involuntary respectfulness of gallantry, and half unconsciously leading her by the hand into my retreat. She yielded, blushing and confused, while I, apologizing, imploring, and gazing with new admiration at every look, unstrapped my basket, placed it in the least exposed corner, spread over it my outside coat, and having thus arranged a seat, (which, however, she did not yet accept,) retired to the opposite side, and reluctantly ceasing to gaze, gave up my whole faculties to wonder – who could she be? Her rich dress, – velvet habit, hat and feathers, – her patrician elegance of beauty and manner, at once proclaimed her rank; but who could there be in Glen— above the homely class to which my host belonged? And his daughter, Miss Janet, was certainly a brilliant of a very different water. But, heavens! how the water is running down from my companion's rich hair, and glistening upon her neck with what a breathing lustre! – "Oh, madam, let me entreat you, as you value your safety, use my handkerchief (and I pulled a muffler from my neck) to bind up and dry your hair. Wrap, I beseech you, your feet in my great-coat; and withdraw farther from the wind and rain."

One by one, notwithstanding her gracious refusals, I carefully fulfilled my prescriptions; and now knelt before her, lapping the skirts and sleeves of my envied coat about the little feet and delicate ankles. Yet it seemed to me that she received my services rather with a grateful condescension, than, as I desired, with frank enjoyment of them. So, pausing a moment to account for such a manner, I recollected, and the recollection covered me with confusion, that I must have been, to say the least, as rough a comrade as any one need wish to meet with under a hedge; for, purposing to leave Ireland in another month for Germany, I had, during the last week, allowed my beard to grow all round; putting off from day to day the forming of the moustache, to which I meant to reduce it, and so had my face, at no time very smooth, now covered from ear to ear with a stubble, long, strong, and black as a shoe-brush. My broad-brimmed hat was battered and dinted into strangely uncouth cavities, and the leaf hung flapping over my brows like a broken umbrella; my jacket was tinselled indeed, but it was with the ancient scales of trout; my leathern overalls were black-glazed and greasy; and my whole equipment bore,

I must confess, the evident signs of an unexceptionable rascal.

Indignant at my unworthy appearance, I put myself upon my mettle; and after drawing my fair companion from her intrenchments of shyness and hauteur, succeeded in engaging her in the fair field of a conversation the most animated and interesting, in which it was ever my good fortune and credit to bear a part. She had at first, indeed, when I began by running a parallel between our positions, explained the circumstances of her being driven thither alone, in a manner so general, and with such evident painfulness of hesitation, that I had hardly expected a few slow commonplaces at the most. Such wit, then, and vivacity, tempered with such dignified discretion, as she evinced when I turned the conversation from what I perceived to be perplexing, were by their unexpectedness doubly delightful.

Time and the tempest swept on equally unheeded; topic induced topic, smile challenged smile, and when at last, in obedience to her wishes, I looked towards the north to see whether the sky were clearing, I only prayed that it might rain on till sunset, when I might accompany her to her home, which, to my surprise, I learned was within a few miles, although I did not ascertain exactly where. My prayers were likely enough to be fulfilled; the sky was still one rush of rain – but, heaven and earth! the river had overflowed its banks above: a broad sheet of water was sailing down the hollow behind; and there we were, no human habitation within sight, in the midst of a tempest, between two rapid rivers, with no better shelter, during the continuance of a Lammas[2] flood, than the hollow of a bank which might be ten feet under water in an hour.

---

[2] Lammas. The beginning of August (when Lammas Fairs were held in Belfast and Ballycastle).

I ran down the back of the hill to the edge of the interposing flood; a stunted tree was in the middle, the fork of which I knew was as high as my shoulder; a mass of weeds and briars was already gathered against it; the water had raised them within a foot of the first branch; then I might still ford a passage; no moment was to be lost; I ran back for the lady, but met her half-way in wild alarm, her head bare, her beautiful hair shaken out into the blast, her hands clasped, and her figure just sinking. I caught her in my arms, and bore her forward with all my speed; but before I again reached the sweeping inundation, insensibility had released her from the terrors of our passage.

I dashed in, holding her across my body, with her head resting on my shoulder; the first step took me to the knee. I raised my burden and plunged forward; the water rose to my haunches. I lifted her again across my breast, rushed on, and sank to the waist. I felt that I could not long support a dead weight in that position; so lowering her limbs into the water, I profited by that relief, and reached the tree.

The flood had now covered me to the breast, and the lady's neck and bosom were all that remained unimmersed. I leaned against the old trunk, and breathed myself. I raised her drooping head on my shoulder, and pressed my cheek to her forehead; but neither lip nor eyelid moved. I could not but gaze upon her face; it lay among the long floating tresses and turbulent eddies, fair as the water's own lily, and as unconscious. My heart warmed to the lovely being, and I bent over her, kissing her lips, and pressing her bosom to mine, with an affection so strangely strong, that I might have stood thus till escape had been impossible, but that the rustling of the rubbish, as it crept up the rugged stump with the rise of the waters, caught my ear – a thunderbolt smouldering at my feet could not have sounded so horrible – all my fresh affections rushed back to my heart in multiplied alarm for the safety of their new-found treasure – I started from my resting-place, and swinging back the long hair from my eyes, once more breasted the stream with clenched teeth and dripping brows. But still as farther I advanced, the water grew deeper and deeper, and the current split upon my shoulder, and twisted through my legs, still stronger and stronger. Lumps of black moss, dried peats, and heavy sods, now struck me, and tumbled on; while wisps of yellow grass and long straws doubled across my body and entangled me. My limbs wavered at every step, as I strained and writhed them through the current. I gave way – I was half lifted – the river and the burn met not a hundred yards below – had I had the strength of ten men, I could not have supported her through that tumult – every step swerved towards the conclusion of at least her existence; yet with love tenfold did I now press her to my heart, and with tenfold energy struggle to make good her rescue – her eyes opened – I murmured prayers, comforts, and endearments – she saw the red torrent around, the tawny breakers before, the black storm overhead; but she saw love in my eye, she heard it in my words; and there, within her probable death-bed, and in the embrace of her probable companion in death, she was wooed among the waters, and was won. Another effort – but the eddy swung me round, and I had given up all as lost, save my interest in that perishing girl; when suddenly I heard, through the dashing of waves and the hissing of rain, the hoarse cry of a man, "Courage – hold up, sir – this way, halloo!"

I turned, half thinking it imagination, but there I really saw a man up to the breast in the flood, supporting with arms and shoulders a powerful black horse which he urged across the current. Another minute, and I stood firm behind the breakwater they formed at my side. My dear charge had again fainted; he assisted me to raise her to the saddle; but suddenly as he looked at her, he uttered a wild cry of astonishment, and kissing and embracing her, exclaimed, "My Madeline, my daughter, my dear child! – Why, sir, how is this?" "Oh, sir, the river is rising a foot a-minute – take the bridle, I beseech you, and let me support the lady and the horse's flank – I will explain all when she is out of danger." So saying, I laid my shoulder to the work and urged him on; we had an easier task, and in another minute succeeded in getting safe out of that perilous passage.

I now looked at our preserver; he was a handsome, tall, and vigorous man, about forty; evidently a soldier and gentleman. He lifted his daughter from the saddle; and while I recounted the particulars of her adventure, unclasped her habit and chafed her forehead; but all was of no avail. He looked distractedly, first at his daughter and then at me; and after a pause of contending emotions, rose, laid her across the pommel, placed his foot in the stirrup, and turning to me said, "I am embarrassed by many cir-cumstances – take my blessings for this day's help – and forget us."

"I can never forget."

"Then take this trifling remembrance." He pulled a ring from his finger and handed it to me; threw himself into the saddle; placed his daughter across his body, and crying, ere I could say a word for sheer amazement, "Farewell, farewell!" and once more, with some emotion, "Farewell, sir, and may God bless you!" put spurs to his horse, and dashed off at full speed for a pass which leads into the wild country of the Misty Braes[3].

Till they disappeared among the hills, I stood watching them from the bank where they had left me, bareheaded, numbed, and indignant; with the rain still pelting on me, and the ring between my fingers. It was a costly diamond; I pitched it after him with a curse, and bent my weary way towards Knowehead, a distance of full five miles, in a maze of uncertainty and speculation. She

[3] The 'Misty Burn' is a district beside a mountain tributary of the Glenwhirry River of the same name.

had not told her name, and she seemed to desire a concealment of her residence; her father's conduct more plainly evinced the same motive; many of the heads of the rebellion were still lurking with their families among the mountains of Ulster; the only house in the direction they had taken, at all likely to be the retreat of respectable persons, was the old Grange of Moyabel; and it was the property of a gentleman then abroad, but connected with all the chief Catholic rebels in the North. All this made me naturally conclude that these were some of that unhappy party; and when I considered that both daughter and father had been riding from different quarters to the same destination – for, as well as I could surmise from her vague account of herself, she had left the servant, behind whom she had come so far, to wait the arrival of her father, who had promised to join them there. I was able to satisfy myself of their being only on their way to Moyabel; and I therefore determined not to create suspicion by making useless enquiries as to the present family there, but to take the first opportunity of judging for myself of the new comers. But how after such a dismissal introduce myself? Here lay the difficulty; and beyond this I could fix on nothing, so with a heavy heart I climbed the hill before my kinsman's house, and presented myself at the wide door of the kitchen, just as the twilight was darkening down into night.

I found my host sitting as was his wont; his nightcap on his head, his long staff in his hand, and two greyhounds at his feet, behind the fire upon his oaken settle. "I'm thinkin', Willie," he began as he saw me enter – "I'm thinkin' ye hae catched a wet sark – Janet, lass, fetch your cusin a dram – Nane o' your piperly smellin' bottles," cried he, as she produced some cordials in an ancient liquor-stand – "Nane o' your auld wife's jaups for ane o' my name – fetch something purpose-like; for when my nevoy has changed himself, we'll hae a stoup o' whisky, and a crack thegither." In a few minutes I was seated in dry clothes, before a bowl of punch and a blazing fire, beside the old gentleman on his oaken sofa. At any other time I would have enjoyed the scene with infinite satisfaction; for the national tipple, in my mind, drinks nowhere so pleasantly as on a bench behind the broad hearth-stone of such a kitchen-hall as my friend's. Our smaller gentry had, it is true, long since betaken themselves to their parlours and their drawing-rooms; and the steams of whisky-punch had already risen with the odours of bohea, and the smoke of seaborne coals, to the damask hangings and alabaster cornices of many high-ceiled and stately apartments. Yet there were still some of the old school, who, like my good friend, continued to make their headquarters, after the ancient fashion, among their own domestics, and behind their own hearth-stone; for in all old houses the fire is six feet at least from the gable, and the space between is set apart for the homely owner.

It was strange, then, that I, who hitherto had so intensely relished such a scene, should be so absent now that it was spread round me in its perfection. The peat and bog-fir fire before me, and the merry faces glistening through the white smoke beyond; the chimney overhead, like some great minster bell (the huge hanging pot for the clapper); the antlers, broadsword, and sporting tackle on the wall behind; the goodly show of fat flitches and briskets around me and above, and that merry and wise old fellow, glass in hand, with endless store of good stories, pithy sayings, and choice points of humour, by my side; yet with all I sat melancholy and ill at ease. In vain did the rare old man tell me his best marvels; how he once fought with Tom Hughes, a wild Welshman, whom he met in a perilous journey through the forests of Cheshire; how Tom would not let go his grip when he had him down ("whilk was a foul villainy;") and how he had to roll into a running water before he could get loose ("whilk shewed the savage natur of thae menseless barbarians.") In vain he told me that pleasant jest, how my grandfather "ance wiled the six excisemen into a lone house, and then gaed in himsell, and pyed them through the windows, whilk cleared the country-side o' that vermin as lang as auld Redrigs was to the fore." In vain he told me how his old dog Stretcher hunted the black hare from Dunmoss to Skyboe. I left him in the subtlest of the doubles, and in another minute was in the penthouse of clay, the river boiling at my feet, and the rain rushing round my head; but before me were the rich delighted eyes and quickening features of my unknown beauty. Again I bore her through the flood; again I bent over her, and pressed her to my breast, and once more in fancy I had felt the thrill of her returned embrace; once more I had kissed her lips, and once more we had vowed to live or die together, when I was startled from my reverie by a question which the unsuspecting old man was now repeating for the third time. I stammered an excuse, and roused myself to the hearing of another excellent jest; but what it might have been I know not, for the entrance of a young labourer, an old acquaintance of my own, with whom he had business, cut it short. "Aleck," he said, "get ready to set out for the fair upon the morn's e'en; and, Aleck, my man, keep yoursell out o' drink and fechtin' – and, my bonny man, I'm saying, the neist time ye gang a courtin' to the Grange, (I pricked up my ears all at once,) see that ye're no ta'en for ane o' thae rebel chiels, wha, they say, are burrowin' e'en noo about the auld wa's as thick as mice in a meal-ark." – "But Aleck," crooned old Mause from the corner, "whilk ane o' the lasses are you for?" This was enough. I watched my opportunity, slipped out to the stable, found Aleck, who had retreated thither in his confusion, and, point-blank, proposed that he should take me with him that very night, and introduce me to one of the girls at Moyabel, as I longed to have an hour's courting after the old fashion before I left the country. I concluded by offering him a handsome consideration, which, however, he refused; but, sitting down in the manger, began to consider, my proposal, with such head-scratching and nail-biting,

as confirmed me in my opinion that there was something myste-
rious about the family of the Grange. "Master William," said he
at last, "I canna refuse ye, and you gaun awa', maybe never to see
a lass o' your ain country again; but ye maun promise never to
speak o' whatever ye may see strange aboot the hoose; for, atween
oursells, there are anes expeckit there this verra night wha's names
wadna cannily bear tellin'; and Jeanie trusts me, and I maunna
beguile her; but the waters are out, and we will hae a lang and
cauld tramp through the bogs, sae get a drap o' somethin' for the
road, and I'll hae Tam Herron's Sunday suit ready for you after
bedtime. Saul! ye'll mak a braw weaver wi' the beard; and wi' a'
your Englified discoorsin', ye can talk as like a Christian as ever
when ye like. – Nanny will think hersell fitted at last; but ye
maunna be ower crouse wi' Nanny, Master William." I promised
every thing; waited impatiently till the family had gone to rest;
found Aleck true to his engagement; put on the clothes he had
prepared, and we stole out about midnight.

It was pitch dark, but fair and calm; so, with the hopes of
getting to our journey's end not wet above the knee, we commenced stumbling and bolting along the great stones and ruts
of the causeway; this we cleared without any accident, farther
than my slipping once into the ditch, and now found ourselves
upon the open hill-side, splashing freely over the soaked turf and
slippery pathway. I was in high spirits, and though squirting the
black puddle to my knees at every step, and seeing no more of
the road I was to travel on than another one in advance, yet faced
onward with great gaiety and good humour. After some time,
however, Aleck began snuffing the air, and, with evident concern,
announced the approach of a mist, which soon thickened into
perceptibility to me also. Our path, which hitherto had swept
across sheep-grazing uplands and grassy knolls, now began to
thread deep rushy bottoms, with here and there a quaking spot
of quagmire, or a mantled stream, which I knew by the cold wa-

ter running sharp below, and by the thick, dull gathering of the weeds about my legs – for the mist made all so dark, that I can only give a blind man's description. The way now became more intricate and broken, but still I followed Aleck cheerily, pushing through all obstacles, and thinking only of the best measures to be taken when we should arrive at Moyabel, when I suddenly perceived that my footsteps were treading down the long wet grass and heavy sedge itself, and that any distinct pathway no longer remained to guide us. I began to doubt Aleck's knowledge of the road, which he still maintained to be unshaken; but the next two steps settled the matter, by bringing us both up to the middle in a running river. We scrambled out without saying a word, Aleck being silent from confusion, and I fearing to increase it by reproaches. He began to grope about for the path we had come by; and finding what he thought our track, pursued it a few steps to the right. I thought I had it to the left, and began to explore in that direction. "Hallo! where are you now?" I cried, as I missed him from my side. He answered "Here," from a considerable distance lower down. "Where?" I repeated. – "Hereawa," he answered.—"Hereawa, thereawa, wandering Willie[4]," I hummed in bitter jollity, as I proceeded in the direction of the voice, "Hereawa, thereawa, haud your way hame," when – squash, crash, bolt, heels over head – plump I went over a brow into a very Devil's Punch-Bowl; for bottom I found none, though shot from the bank with the impetus of an arrow. Down I went, the water closing over me in strata and substrata, each one colder than the other, till I expected to find my head at last clashing against the young ice wedges of a preternatural frost below. I sunk at least fifteen feet before I could collect my energies and turn. I thought I would never reach the top. To it at last I came, sputtering, blown, and fairly frightened. I never waited to consider my course, but

---

[4] "Wandering Willie", Robert Burns 1793.

striking desperately out, swam straight forward, till I came bump against the bank. I clambered up, and listened. The first sound I could distinguish, after the bubbling and hissing left my ears, was Aleck's voice nearly before me, on the opposite side. He was singing out something between a howl and a halloo; for he also had got into the water, and could not find bottom any where but on the spot he occupied. He could not swim a stroke. There was nothing for it but to go back and rescue him. The unexpectedness alone of my first dip had caused my confusion. That was gone off, and I again plunged resolutely into the river, which I now could discern grey in the clearing mist. A few strokes brought me to where the poor fellow stood, with his arms extended upon the water, and his neck stretched to the utmost to keep it out of his mouth. I knew the danger of taking an alarmed man of greater weight and strength than myself upon my back; and therefore, comforting him with assurances of safety, I tried, in all directions, for bottom, which at last I found, and having sounded the bed of the river to the opposite side, returned, and with some difficulty succeeded in guiding and supporting him across.

The mist was now rapidly thinning away, and I could distinguish the high bank black against the sky. It was a joyful sight, and induced, by a natural association, the pleasant thought of the comforter in my pocket, I took a mighty dram: then feeling for Aleck's head, (he had lain down, streaming like Father Nile in the pictures, among the rushes at my feet), I directed the bottle's mouth to his. He had been making his moan in an under whine ever since I first heard him lamenting his condition on the opposite side; but no sooner did his lips feel the smooth insinuator's presence, than (his tongue being put out of the way) they closed with instinctive affection, and went together when the long embrace was past, with a smack quite cheering. Then slowly rising, and fetching a deep sigh as he gathered himself together, "Lord, Lord," said he, "I'm nane the waur o' that. But, Master

William, to tell God's truth, I dinna ken whaur we are. That we hae crossed Glen— water, or the Hillhead burn, or the Marcher's dyke, I'm positive sure; but whilk I'm no just equal to say – but there's somethin' black atween us and the lift; I judge it to be Dunmoss Cairn: let's haud on to it, and we maun soon come to biggit wa's." So saying, he led me forward in the direction of what seemed to me also a distant hill; but being occupied in placing my footsteps, I had ceased to look at it, when all at once there was a crush of leaves about my head, and I found myself under a green tree. "When will this weary night of error have an end?" I mentally exclaimed; but was surprised by Aleck taking my hand, rubbing the palm along the rough stem, and asking in an elate tone what I felt? "A damnably rough bark," growled I; "what do you mean?" He cut a caper full three feet into the air. "Here is a pleasant occurrence now – this rascal is drunk – he will roll into the next ditch and suffocate – I shall be the death of the poor fellow – I shall lose" – here he broke my agreeable meditations. "I'll tell you how it was, Master William; Jeanie and I were partners at the shearin', ("Evidently drunk," thought I,) and I canna tell how it was, ("I well believe you – you can not – but 'twas all my own folly," I muttered,) but I found the maid in a sair fluster that e'en when we parted: ("You'll be in sorer fluster presently if I begin to you – you drunken idiot!" was my running commentary,) and sae just as I came by this auld thorn" – "Then you *do* know where you are – do you?" I cried aloud. – "Sure enough," said he, "for didn't I carve my heart wi' Jeanie's heuk stuck out through it that very night; and isna it here to this minute?" – "Oh, ho, lead on then, in God's name; but tell me where we are, and how far we have to go." – "Why," said he, "the bridge is just a step overby that we ought to hae crossed; and troth, I wonner a dishfu' at mysell for no kennin' the black moss and the dolochan's hole that we hae just come through; for I hae cut turf in the ane, and weshed in the ither, since I was the bouk o' a peat – but here we are at the

end o' the causey that will take us to the Grange." We entered on
a raised and moated bank, which crossed a mossy flat to the old
house; but ere we had advanced a dozen steps, there suddenly
appeared a light moving about, and giving occasional glimpses
of the white walls and thick trees at the further end; it then came
steadily and swiftly towards us; I could presently distinguish the
dull beat of hoofs on the greensward, and soon after, the figures
of two mounted men.

The sides of the old moat were overgrown with furze and
brambles, and we stole into this cover as they approached. The
foremost bore the light, was armed at all points, and mounted
on a fresh horse. I started with exultation where I lay – he was
her father. His companion's black breeches and canting seat proclaimed a priest. They were conversing as they passed. "Another
month, good father, and we will be behind the bastions of Belle
Isle; were it not for my Madeline's sake, I would make it six; but
this bloodhound having been slipped upon us" – The sounds
were here lost in the trampling of their horses; I heard the man
of masses mumble something in reply, and they wheeled out of
hearing up the rugged pathway to the bridge. "Now mind your
promise, Master William," said Aleck, as we rose and proceeded
to the house. We soon arrived there; and he led me to a low wing,
repeating his cautions, and, in answer to my questions, denying
all knowledge of the strangers. Placing me behind a low wall,
he now stole forward, and tapped at a window, and presently I
heard the inmates moving and whispering. The door was soon
opened, and a parley took place, in which I heard my assumed
name made honourable mention of by my intruder. He led me
forward, pushed me gently before him, and I found myself in a
dark passage, soft hands welcoming me, and warm breath playing
on my cheek.

The door was closed, and we were led into a wide rude apartment, dim in the low glow of a heap of embers. A splinter of

bogwood was soon kindled, and by its light I saw that we had been conducted by two girls. One, whom from her attention to Aleck I concluded to be her of the reaping-hook, was a pretty interesting soft maiden. The other, however, had attractions of a very different class: fine-featured, dark-eyed, coal-black-haired and tall; as she stood, her right hand holding the rude torch over her head, while the left gathered the folds of a long cloak under her bosom, with her eyes of coy expectation and merry amazement, she seemed more the ideal of a robber's daughter in some old romance, than a menial in a moorland farm-house. I attempted to salute her, but she held me at bay with her hand. "Hech, lad! ye're no blate – is it knievin' troots* ye think ye are? But, my stars! ye *are* as droukit as if ye had been through a' the pools o' the burn! Sit down, my jo, till we dry ye; and be qu'et till I get a fire." Peats and bogwood were now heaped upon the broad stone, she began puffing away with her pretty puckered mouth; partly, I suppose, because there are no bellows in Glen—; and partly, I took it for granted, to afford me an opportunity of kneeling beside and preeing it. The smoke now rose before me in thick volumes, and for a while I lost sight of Aleck and his Jeanie. By and by, however, on raising my head, I started back at seeing a figure the most extraordinary standing at the further end of the apartment. A blanket covered the shoulders; the feet and legs were bare; a red handkerchief was tied about the head; and, strangest of all, although the hairy neck and whiskers argued him a man, yet was he from the waist to the knees clad in a petticoat!

[* "Knieving trouts" (they call it tickling in England) is good sport. You go to a stony shallow at night, a companion bearing a torch; then, stripping to the thighs and shoulders, wade in; grope with your hands under the stones, sods, and other harbourage, till you find your game, then grip him in your "knieve," and toss him ashore.]

I remember, when a boy, carrying the splits for a servant of the family, called Sam Wham. Now Sam was an able young fellow, well-boned and willing; a hard-headed cudgel-player, and a marvellous tough wrestler, for he had a backbone like a sea-serpent; this gained him the name of the Twister and Twiner. He had got into the river, and with his back to me, was stooping over a broad stone, when something bolted from under the bank on which I stood, right through his legs. Sam fell with a great splash upon his face, but in falling jammed whatever it was against the stone. "Let go, Twister," shouted I, "'tis an otter, he will nip a finger off you." – "Whisht," sputtered he, as he slid his hand under the water; "May I never read a text again, if he isna a sawmont wi' a shouther like a hog!" – " Grip him by the gills, Twister," cried I. – " Saul will I!" cried the Twiner; but just then there was a heave, a roll, a splash, a slap like a pistol-shot; down went Sam, and up went the salmon, spun like a shilling at pitch and toss, six feet into the air. I leaped in just as he came to the water; but my foot caught between two stones, and the more I pulled the firmer it stuck. The fish fell in a spot shallower than that from which he had leaped. Sam saw the chance, and tackled to again: while I, sitting down in the stream as best I might, held up my torch, and cried fair play, as shoulder to shoulder, throughout and about, up and down, roll and tumble, to it they went, Sam and the salmon. The Twister was never so twined before. Yet through crossbuttocks and capsizes innumerable, he still held on; now haled through a pool; now baling up a bank; now heels over head; now head over heels; now head and heels together; doubled up in a corner; but at last stretched fairly on his back, and foaming for rage and disappointment; while the victorious salmon, slapping the stones with his tail, and whirling the spray from his shoulders at every roll, came boring and snoring up the ford. I tugged and strained to no purpose; he dashed by me with a snort, and slid into the deep water. Sam now staggered forward with battered bones and peeled elbows, blowing like a grampus, and cursing like nothing but himself. He extricated me, and we limped home. Neither rose for a week; for I had a dislocated ankle, and the Twister was troubled with a broken rib. Poor Sam! he had his brains discovered at last by a poker in a row, and was worm's meat within three months; yet, ere he died, he had the satisfaction of feasting on his old antagonist, who was man's meat next morning. They caught him in a net, Sam knew him by the twist in his tail.]

I started to my feet, visions of sleepwalkers and lunatics thronging hearth; and kneeling down upon the through my imagination, but was caught hold of by Nanny, who, shaking with suppressed laughter, whispered me, while the tears ran out and danced upon her long lashes for very fun, that it was only precious Aleck, "wham Jeanie had cled in her bit wyliecoat, since she dauredna wake the hoose to look for aught else;" then, laying her hand upon my shoulder (and the wet oozed from between her fingers), she proposed, with a maidenly mixture of kindliness and hesitation, that I should go and do so likewise. Who knows how I might have stood the temptation, had she not in time perceived my error, and, blushing deeply, explained, that as Aleck had done – undressed himself alone – so should I. Under these stipulations, I declined parting with more than my coat, for which she substituted a curiously quilted coverlet; then bringing me warm water, insisted on my bathing my feet. I gladly consented; but hardly had I pulled off the coarse stockings, and washed the black soil from my hands, when there began a grievous coughing and grumbling in the room from which the girls had come.

"Lord, haud a grip o' us!" cried Aleck; "it's auld *Peg* hoastin' – De'il wauken her, the cankered rush! she'll breed a bonny splore gin she finds me here."

"Whisht, whisht," whispered Nanny, "she's as keen as colly i' the lugs; and glegger than baudrons i' the dark."

The libelled Mistress Margaret gave no farther time for calumniation; slamming open the door, she came down upon us, gaunt, grim, and unescapable – "Ye menseless tawpies! ye bauld cutties! ye wanton limmers! ye – *wha's this?*" She snatched the light from Nannie's hand, and poked it close to my face – "Wha's this? I say, wha's this?"

"Hoots, woman!" cried Nanny, spiritedly, yet with an air of conciliation, "I'se bail ye mony a boy has come over the moss to crack wi' yoursell when ye were a lassie."

"*When* I was a lassie!"

I thought she would have choked; but her indignation at last made its way up in thunder upon my devoted head.

"Wha are ye? what are ye? what fetches ye sornin' here? ye" —

Nanny again interposed. "He's just a weaver lad, I tell ye, that Aleck Lowther fetched frae the Langslap Moss to keep him company."

"A weaver lad!" (I had raised my foot to the rim of the tub, and sat with my chin upon my hand, and my elbow on my knee, laughing, to the great aggravation of her anger).

"A weaver lad! – there's niver a wabster o' the Langslap Moss wi' siccan a leg as that! – there's ne'er a ane o' a' the creeshy clan wha's shins arena bristled as red as a belly rasher! – there's ne'er a wabster o' the Langslap Moss wi' the track o' a ring upon his wee finger! – there's ne'er a wabster o' the Langslap Moss wi' aughteen hunner linen in his sark-frill! – Jamie, hoi! Jamie Steenson, here's a spy!"

So sudden and overpowering was her examination and judgment, and her voice had risen to such a pitch of clamour, that all my attempts at interruption and explanation were lost; while the screams which the girls could not control when they heard her call in assistance, prevented a reply. One after another, five ruffianly-looking fellows rushed in at her call; and ere I could free myself from the importunate exculpations of poor Nanny, they were crowding and cursing round me; while one, apparently their leader, held a lantern to my face, a pike to my throat, and demanded my name and business. That these were one unhappy remnant of the rebel party I could not doubt; if I declared my real name, I might expect all that exasperation could prompt and desperation execute against a disguised enemy in the camp; (for the only one from whom I could expect protection was, as I had seen, beyond my appeal.) Again, to give a fictitious name, and keep up the character of a country weaver, was revolting to my pride, and in all likelihood beyond my ability. Which horn of this dilemma I might have impaled myself on, I cannot tell; for a sudden interruption prevented my answer.

Aleck, who had with difficulty been hitherto restrained by the united exertions of the three women, here burst from their arms, tossed off his blanket, and leaped with a whoop into the middle of the floor; – except the short petticoat about his loins he was stark naked. "I'm twal stane wecht – my name's Aleck Lawther – I'll slap ony man o' ye for four-an'-twenty tens!" As he uttered this challenge, tossing his long arms about his head, bouncing upright, and cutting like a posture-master at the end of every clause, while the scanty kilt fluttered and flapped about his sinewy hams, the men fell back in a panic, as if from a spectre; but their astonishment soon gave place to indignation, and my questioner, clubbing his pike, stepped forward, and making the shaft rattle off the white array of ribs, which poor Aleck's flourish had left unprotected, reduced his proposals to practice in a trice. He, wisely making up for disparity of forces by superiority of weapon, started back, and adroitly unhooking the long iron chain and pot-hooks from the chimney, set them flying round his head like a slinger of old; and meeting his antagonist with a clash, shot him rocket-wise into the corner: then giving another whirl to his stretcher, and leaping out with the full swing of his long body, he brought it to bear upon the next. There was another clattering crash, and the man went down; but pitching with his shoulder into the tub, upset it, and sent a flood of water into the fire. Smoke, steam, and white ashes, whirled up in clouds; the lantern was trampled out, and the battle became general: for one rascal, lifting his fallen comrade's pike, (there was luckily but one among them,) advanced upon me. I had just light to see the thrust, and parry it. Another second, and we had closed in the midst of that strange atmosphere, striking and sneezing at each other across the pike shaft, as we each strove to wrest it to himself. My antagonist was a lusty fellow, and tugged me stoutly, while I kept him between me and the main fight, now raging through the water and the fire: this I could just distinguish among the vapour and smoke, dashed about in red showers of embers, as each new tramp and whirl of the combatants swept it from the hearthstone. How Aleck fought his two opponents I could not imagine; yet once, during a minute's relaxation on our parts, when, having got the pike jammed between a table and the wall, we were reduced to the by-play of kicking one another's shinbones, I could hear, every now and again, above the medley of curses and screams, (for the women were all busy,) his lusty "Hah!" as he put in each successive blow; and then the bolt and thud of some one gone down, far away in the distance; or the rush of a capsize among the loose lumber at my feet. But I had no longer an opportunity of noting his prowess; for my antagonist, getting the weapon disentangled, hauled me after him into the open floor, and then began upon the swinging system. So away we went, sweeping down chairs and stools, and rolling fallen bodies over in our course; till tired and dizzy, I suddenly planted myself, let go both holds, and dashing in right and left together, sent him whirling like a comet, impetuous and hot, into the void beyond. But my own head here fell heavily upon my breast; and the whole scene, smoke, fire, and shifting shapes, with all their mingled hissing, and battering, oaths, shrieks, and imprecations, shut upon my senses.

A Babel of dull sound, chiming and sawing within my head, announced my returned consciousness. This is no dream, thought

I; I have been hurt, but I am afraid to ask myself where. If my skull should be fractured now, and I should be an idiot all my life, or if my arm should be broken – farewell to the river! But can I be still doubled up among those pots and pans which I crushed beneath me in my fall? No, – dark as it is, I feel that I am laid straight and soft. I must be in bed, but where? where? It was some time before I had courage to confirm my doubts of my head's condition: it was carefully bandaged, and doubtless much shattered: I could feel that I was in a close-paneled bedstead, such as are usual in old houses; but had too much discretion to attempt the hazardous experiment of rising without knowing either my strength or situation. So I lay, fancying all sorts of means to account for my preservation: need I say that the main agent in all was the fair Madeline?

My curiosity was at length relieved; a rude folding-door opened opposite, and shewed a low dim sitting-room beyond, from which there rose a few steps to the entrance of my chamber. On these appeared, not, alas! the fancied visitant who was to flit about my bedside, and mix her bright presence with my dreams; but stately and severe, with a pale cheek and compressed lip, her father – my aversion.

I lay silent, sick at the thoughts of my own meanness in his eyes; while he advanced, shading the light of the candle from my face, and in a low cold tone, asked if 1 desired anything?

I shall never forget him as he stood, the light thrown full upon his strong features and broad chest, and shining purple through the fingers of his large hand. "I asked, sir, did you require any assistance?" he repeated. "Are you in pain?" he went on. I now replied that my chief pain was caused by my own unworthy appearance; made a confused apology for my misconduct, and offered my acknowledgments for the protection I had received. "You have saved the life of my child," he said, turning slightly from me, "and protection is a debt which must be paid; for your follower, he must thank the same circumstance for what little life his own mad conduct has left him." Without another word, he took a phial from the table, and, pouring out a draught, handed it to me. I mechanically drunk it off; but ere I had taken it from my lips, he was gone. I heard the doors close and the bolts shoot after him with strange forebodings; and when the sound of his footsteps had died away in the long passage beyond, fell back in a wild maze of apprehension and self censure, till I again sank into a heavy sleep.

When I awoke, there was a yellow twilight in my little cabin, from the scattering of a red ray of the sunset which streamed through a crevice in the door. I had therefore slept a whole day; my fever was abated; the gnawing pain had left my head, and I longed to eat. I knocked upon the boards, and the door was presently opened; but it was some time ere my eyes could endure the flood of light which then burst in. The figure which at length became visible amid it, was little worthy so goodly a birth. The lank, slack, ill-hinged anatomy of Peg, with a bottle in one hand, and a long horn spoon in the other, advanced, and in no gracious tone demanded what was my will. I turned and lay silent; for I never felt an awkward situation so embarrassing as then. My gorge rose at the malignant cause of all my disasters; but interest and discretion told me to be civil if I spoke at all. I gave no answer; she was in no humour to suffer such trifling with her time. "Hear till him, Jamie!" she exclaimed to some one behind her, "hear till him, the fashious scunner! he dunts folk frae their wark as if he was the laird o' the Lang Marches himsell, and then "Good Mistress Margaret". Mistress me nae mistresses! there's ne'er a wife i' the parish has a right to be mistressed, since she deeit wha's wean ye wad betray! Deil hae me gin I can keep my knieves aff ye, ye ill-faured bluid-seller!" – "Ill-faured *what?*" shouted I. "No just ill-faured neither, blest be the Maker, and mair's the pity; ye're a clean boy eneugh, as I weel may say, wha had the strippin' and streekin' o' ye; but I say that ye're just a bluid-seller, a reform-er, a spy, gin ye like it better!" She backed down the steps, and holding a leaf of the door at each side, stretched in her neck, and went on, "Aye, spy, Willie Macdonnell, spy to your teeth. – Isna your name upon your sark breast? and arena the arms that ye disgrace upon your seal, and daur ye deny them? daur ye deny that ye're the swearer away o' the innocent bluid o' puir Hughy Morrison, wham ye hangit like a doug upon the lamp-posts o' Doonpatrick? Daur ye hae the face to deny that ye come here e'en noo to reform upon Squarc O'More and his bonny wean? Daur ye hae the impurence to deny it?" Here I was relieved by the entrance of Mr O'More himself. I addressed him in a tone as cool and conciliatory as I could command. "I am much relieved to find, sir, that any harshness I may have to complain of, has originated in a mistake. I am Mr Macdonnell of Redrigs. It was only last week that I returned from England. I have not been in this part of the country for many years; and can only say, that if any person bearing my name deserves the character you seem to impute to me, I detest him as cordially as you do." He eyed me with visibly increased disgust. "It will not pass, sir, it will not pass. I have had notice of your intentions. Mr Macdonnell of Redrigs is in Oxford." – "I tell you, sir, he is here!" I cried, starting up in bed. "Back, back!" he exclaimed to the servants who were press-ing round; they fell back, and he came up to me. "Hark ye, sir, instead of assuming a name to which you have no right" – The passion which had been burning within me all along, blazed out in uncontrollable fury. I started with a sudden energy out into the floor; dashed backwards and forwards through the room, stamping with indignation, while I asserted my honour, and demanded satisfaction; but the fire which had for a minute animated me failed; my tongue became confused and feeble; the whole scene whirled and flickered round me, and I sunk exhausted, and in a burning fever, on a seat.

Every one who has suffered fever knows what a fiery trance it is. How long mine had continued I could not guess; when the crisis came, it was favourable, and I awoke, cool and delighted, from a long sweet sleep. That scene I had already witnessed, of sunset through the room beyond, was again before me; the same grey and purple haze hung over the mountain, and the same rich sky from above lit up the river-reaches; the dim old room was warm in the mellow light; the folding-doors stood wide open, but on the steps where the marrer of the whole had stood before, lo! the radiance revelling through her hair; the rich light flushing warm through the outline of her face and neck; the sweet repose of satisfaction and conscious care beaming over her whole countenance; benign and beautiful stood Madeline O'More, her finger on her lips. "She, too, thinks me a spy," I muttered, in the bitterness of my heart, and hid my face upon the pillow. But who can describe my delight when I heard her well-remembered accents murmur beside me, "Oh no, believe me, indeed I do not!" I looked up. She was covered with blushes – I felt them reflected on my own cheek – there was a conscious pause. "Then you do believe that I am what I have told you?" I said at last. "Oh yes! but indeed you must forgive the error," she replied; and readily did I admit its justifiableness, when she went on to tell me that a friend had ridden a long journey to warn them against a person bearing my name, and answering to my appearance, an apostate from their own cause, and a noted spy, who, upon some vague information of their retreat, had set out with the intention of discovering and betraying them; and that their friend (in whom I at once recognised the priest I had seen her father conduct from the house) had left them but a few minutes before I arrived. It was now my turn to apologize and explain. She listened, with many pleas of palliation for the indignities I had endured, to my account of my business in Ireland, and the circumstances which had led me to Glen—; but when I came to account for my appearance at

Moyabel, her confusion satisfied me that the motive was already known. I felt suddenly conscious of having been dreaming about her: and I knew that a fevered man's dream is his nurse's perquisite: dissimulation, after what I knew and suspected to have passed, would have been as impossible as repugnant. So then and there, among that mellow sunset in the sick chamber, I confessed to her how my whole thoughts had been haunted by her image, since the time when her father had hurried her from the scene of our meeting; how I could not rest while any scheme, how wild soever, promised me even a chance of again beholding her; how this had induced me to snatch at the first opportunity of discovering her, and had brought on that disastrous adventure which had ended in my wound: but that I still endured another, which I feared would prove incurable, if I might not live upon the hope (and I took her hand) of gaining her to be my heart's physician constantly.

Footsteps suddenly sounded in the passage. I released her hand, and she hid her confusion, in a hasty escape through a side-door, just before her father made his appearance at that of the hall. He advanced with a frank expression of pleasure and concern; took his seat by my bedside; congratulated me on the favourable issue of my illness, and repeated those apologies and explanations which his daughter had already made; adding that his first intention had been to detain me prisoner, so that I could have no opportunity of betraying them until their departure for France; but that the moment he had heard my undisguised ravings, he perceived the injustice of which he had been guilty; that Aleck's speech having returned soon after, (for the poor fellow was so beaten that he could not say a word for three days—but I have taken good care of him,) another evidence, however unnecessary, was afforded by his declaration; and that, therefore, a messenger was immediately dispatched to Knowehead, with private letters, explaining our situation and its causes, and resting on the honour of my friend for the security of all. The trust had been well reposed: Aleck, who

was able to go home in a few days, had come the night before
(although returned that morning) with the intelligence of the real
spy having applied for information to the old gentleman; but that,
loyal subject and zealous protestant as he was, he had given him
no more than a civil indication of his door. All this he told with a
gratified and grateful air, and left me to a night of happy dreams.

Next morning, however, he came to me, and in a serious, nay
severe manner, told me, that as I had divulged the motive which
brought me thither in my ravings, he felt it a duty to himself and
to me, now that I was established in my recovery, to inform me
that, while he forgave my intrusion on a privacy he had already
begged me not to break, he must desire that there should be no
recurrence of attentions to his daughter, which might distract a
heart destined either for the service of a free Catholic in regener-
ated Ireland, or for that of Heaven in a nunnery.

He had laid his hand upon the table, and it unconsciously rest-
ed upon the seals of my watch. "Look," said I, "at these trinkets;
I shall tell you what they are, and let them be my answer. That
rude silver seal, with the arms and initials, was dug from my father's orchard, along with the bones of his ancestor, who fell there
beneath the knives of free Catholics, in '41[5], a grey haired man,
among the seven bodies of his murdered wife and children. Look
again at that curious ring; it was worn by his son, the sole survivor
of all that ancient family who escaped, a maimed and famished
spectre, out of Derry, after the same party had driven him to eat
his sword belt for hunger. Look once again at this more antique
locket; it contains the hair of a maternal ancestor, who perished
for the faith among the fagots of Smithfield; and look, here, at my
own arm, that wound I received when a child, from a the chief of
a 'Heart of Steel' banditti, who, under the same banner, lighted
our family's escape from rape and massacre, by the flames of their

[5] 1641 rebellion.

own burning roof-tree; and yet I – I, every drop of whose blood might well cry out for vengeance, when I see these remembrancers of my wrongs in the hands of my wrongs' defender, do yet take that hand, and long to call him father."

I was here interrupted by the sudden entrance of a splashed and wearied messenger: advancing with a military salute, he presented a letter to Mr O'More. – "Pardon me," he said, hastily tearing it open, "this is on a matter of life and death." He read it in great agitation; led the messenger aside; gave some hurried orders; took down his arms from the mantelpiece; and drawing his belt, and fixing in his pistols while he spoke, addressed me: – "Notwithstanding what you have urged, my determination remains unaltered. I must leave Moyabel, for I cannot now say how long: you shall be taken care of in my absence: farewell, sir, farewell." He shook me by the hand, and hurried away. I heard confusion in the house, and thought I could distinguish the sweet voice of Madeline, broken by sobs at his departure. A considerable party seemed to leave the house; for there was a great trampling of horses in the court-yard, and two or three mounted men passed by the windows. At length they were out of hearing, and I determined not to lose another minute of the precious opportunity. My clothes had been brought from Knowehead, and I was so much recovered that I found myself able to rise, and set about dressing immediately. My continental visions of beard were more than realized; and if I failed to produce a shapely moustache, 'twas not for lack of material. With fluttering expectation, I selected the most graceful of the pantaloons; drew on my rings; arrayed myself in the purple velvet slippers, cap, and brocade dressing-gown; took one lingering last look at the little mirror, and descended into the parlour. I drew a writing-table to me, and penned a long letter to Knowehead; another to Redrigs, and had half-finished a sonnet to Madeline. The day was nearly past, and she had not yet made her appearance.

For the first time the thought struck me, and that with a pang which made me leap to my feet, that she had accompanied her father, and was gone! gone, perhaps, to a nunnery in France! gone, and lost to me for ever! "Hilloa, Peg!" and I thumped the floor with the poker, "Peg, I say! as you would not have me in another fever, come here!" She came to the door: the poor old creature's eyes were swollen and bloodshot: she made a frightened courtesy to me as I stood, the papers crumpled up in one hand, and the poker in the other. – "Peggy, oh, Peggy! where is your young mistress?"

"Save us, your honour! Ye are na weel; sall 1 fetch you a drap cordial?"

"Your mistress? your mistress? where is your young mistress?"

"Oh, sir, dear! take anither posset, and gang to your bed."

"To the devil I pitch your posset! where is your young mistress? where is Madeline O'More?"

She turned to escape: I leaped forward, and caught her by the shoulder – "Since ye maun ken, then," she screamed, "by God's providence, she's on the saut water wi' the Square, her father." I sank back upon the sofa. "Wha," she continued in a soothing strain, "has left me to take charge o' your honour's head till ye can gang your lane: A' the ithers are awa, but wee Jeanie and mysell; and ye wadna, surely your honour wadna gang to frichten twa lane weemen, by dwamin' awa that gait, and deein' amang their hands? But save us, if there's no auld Knowehead himsell, wi' that bauld sorner, Aleck Lawther, on a sheltie at his heels, trottin' doon the causey! – Jeanie, hoi, Jeanie, rin and open the yett."

I lay back – sick – sick – sick. The old man, booted and spurred, strode in –

"I'm thinkin', Willie, ye hae catched a cloured head?"

"If I do not catch a strait-waistcoat, sir, it will be the less matter."

"Willie, man," said he, without noticing my comment, "she's

weel awa, and you are weel redd – but toss off thae wylie-coats and nightcaps, and lap yoursell up in mensefu' braidclaith; for, donsie as you are, you maun come alang wi' me to Knowehead – there's a troop o' dragoons e'en now on Skyboe side, wi' your creditable namesake at their head, and they'll herry Moyabel frae hearth-stane to riggin' before sax hours are gane – best keep frae under a lowin' king-post, and on the outside o' the four wa's o' a prevost. – You're no fit to ride, man; and you couldna thole the joltin' o' a wheel-car – but never fear, we'll slip you hame upon a feather-bed – Nae denial, Willie - here, draw on your coat: now, that's somethin' purpose-like – cram thae flim-flams into a poke, my bonny Jean, and fetch me a handkerchief to tie about his head: Come, Willie, take my arm – come awa, come awa."

I was passive in his hands, for I felt as weak as an infant. They wrapped me up in great-coats and blankets, and supported me to the courtyard. I had hardly strength to speak to Aleck, whom I now saw for the first time since the night of his disaster; the poor fellow's face still bore the livid marks of his punishment, but he was active and assiduous as ever. A slide car or slipe – a vehicle something like a Lapland sledge was covered with bedding in the middle of the square: a cart was just being hurried off, full of loose furniture, with Peggy and Jenny in front. I was placed upon my hurdle, apparently as little for this world as if Tyburn had been its destination: Knowehead and Aleck mounted their horses; took the reins of that which drew me at either side, and hauled me off at a smart trot along the smooth turf of the grass-grown causeway. The motion was sliding and agreeable, except on one occasion, when we had to take a few perches of the highway in crossing the river; but when we struck off into the green horse-track again, and began to rise and sink upon the ridges of the broad lea, I could have compared my humble litter to the knight's horses, which felt like proud seas under them. From the sample I had had of that part of the country on the night of the flood, I had anticipated a "confused march forlorn, through bogs, caves, fens, lakes, dens, and shades of death,[6]" but was agreeably surprised to see the Longslap Moss a simple stripe along the water's edge, lying dark in the deepening twilight, a full furlong from our path, which, instead of weltering through the soaked and spungy flats that I had expected, wound dry and mossy up the gentle slope of a smooth green hill; so that, although the night closed in upon us ere half our journey was completed, we arrived at Knowehead without farther accident than one capsize, (the beauty of slipping consists in the impossibility or breaks down,) and so far from being the worse of my "sail," I felt actually stronger than on leaving the Grange; nevertheless I was put to bed, where I continued for a week.

Next day brought intelligence of the wrecking of Moyabel in the search for the rebel general and the sick Frenchman: Our measures had been so well taken, however, that no suspicion attached itself to Knowehead. I learned from Peggy, so soon as her lamentations subsided, that Mr O'More was a south country gentleman, who had married her master's sister, and that Madeline was his only child; that this had been his first visit to the north since the death of his lady, which had taken place at her brother's house, but that Moyabel had long been the resort of his friends and emissaries. The old woman left Knowehead that night, and I learned no more; for Jenny (who remained with Miss Janet) had been so busy with her care of Aleck during his illness, and afterwards so unwell herself, that she knew nothing more than I.

Another week completely re-established me in my strength; but the craving that had never left me since the last sight of Madeline,

---

[6] Milton's *Paradise Lost*: "In confused march forlorn, th' adventurous bands, / ... Through many a dark and dreary vale / They passed, and many a region dolorous, / O'er many a frozen, many a fiery alp, / Rocks, caves, lakes, fens, bogs, dens, and shades of death —".

kept me still restless and impatient. Meanwhile Aleck's courtship had ripened in the golden sun of matrimony, and the wedding took place on the next Monday morning. He was a favourite with all at Knowehead, and the event was celebrated by a dance of all the young neighbours. After witnessing the leaping and flinging in the barn for half an hour, I retired to Miss Janet's parlour, where I was lolling away the evening on her high-backed sofa, along with the old gentleman, who, driven from his capitol in the kitchen by the bustle of the day, had installed himself in the unwonted state of an embroidered armchair beside me. We were projecting a grand coursing campaign before I should leave the country, and listening to the frequent bursts of merriment from the barn and kitchen, when little Davie came in to tell his master that "Paul Ingram was speerin' gain he wad need ony tay, or brendy, or prime pigtail, or Virginney leaf."

"I do not just approve of Paul's line of trade," observed the old man, turning to me; "for I'm thinking his commodities come oftener frae the smuggler's cave than the King's store; but he's a merry deevil, Paul, and has picked up a braw hantle o' mad ballads ae place and another; some frae Glen— here, some frae Galloway, some frae the Isle o' Man, and some queer lingos he can sing, that he says he learned frae the Frenchmen."

A sudden thought struck me. "I will go out and get him to sing some to me, sir." – "Is Rab Halliday there, Davie?" enquired he.

"Oh aye, sir," said Davie; "it's rantin' Rab that ye hear roarin' e'en noo."

"Weel, tell him, Davie, that here's Mr William, wha has learned to speel Parnassus by a step-ladder, has come to hear the sang he made about my grandmither's wooin'."

Accordingly Davie ushered me to the kitchen. I could distinguish through the reaming fumes of liquor and tobacco about half a dozen carousers; they were chorusing at the full stretch of their lungs the song of a jolly fellow in one corner, who, nodding, winking, and flourishing his palms, in that state of perfect bliss "that good ale brings men to," was lilting up

> "Till the house be rinnin' round about,
> It's time enough to flit;
> When we fell, we aye gat up again,
> And sae will we yet!"

This was ranting Rab Halliday – they all rose at my entrance; but being able to make myself at home in all companies, I had little difficulty in soon restoring them to their seats and jollity; while Davie signified what was to him intelligible of his master's wishes to the tuneful ranter. Rab, after praying law for any lack of skill that might be detected by my learning, sang with great humour the following verses, which he entitled:

The Canny Courtship

Young Redrigs walks where the sunbeams fa';
He sees his shadow slant up the wa' –
Wi' shouthers sae braid, and wi' waist sae sma',
*   Guid faith he's a proper man!*
He cocks his cap, and he streeks out his briest;
And he steps a step like a lord at least;
And he cries like the devil to saddle his beast,
*   And off to court he's gaun.*
The Laird o' Largy is far frae hame,
But his dochter sits at the quiltin' frame,
Kamin' her hair wi' a siller kame,
*   In mony a gowden ban':*
Bauld Redrigs loups frae his blawin' horse,
He prees her mou' wi' a freesome force –
'Come take me Nelly, for better for worse,
*   To be your ain guidman.'*

'I'll no be harried like bumbee's byke –
I'll no be handled unleddy like –
I winna hae ye, ye worryin' tyke,
   The road ye came gae 'lang!'
He loupit on wi' an awesome snort,
He bang'd the fire frae the flinty court;
He's aff and awa in a snorin' sturt,
   As hard as he can whang.
It's doon she sat when she saw him gae,
And a' that she could do or say,
Was – 'O! And alack! And a well-a-day!
   I've lost the best guidman!'
But if she was wae, it's he was wud;
He garr's them a' frae his road to scud;
But Glowerin' Sam gied thud for thud,
   And then to the big house ran.
The Glowerer ran for the kitchen dorr;
Bauld Redrigs hard at his heels, be sure,
He's wallop'd him roun' and roun' at the floor,
   As wha but Redrigs can?
Then Sam he loups to the dresser shelf –
'I daur ye wallop my leddy's delf;
I daur ye break but a single skelf
   Frae her cheeny bowl, my man!'
But Redrigs' bluid wi' his hand was up;
He'd lay them neither for crock nor cup,
He play'd awa' wi' his cuttin' whup,
   And doon the dishes dang;
He clatter'd them doon, sir, raw by raw;
The big anes foremost, and syne the sma';
He came to the cheeny cups last o' a' –
   They glanced wi' gowd sae thrang!
Then bonny Nelly came skirlin' butt;

Her twa white arms roun his neck she put –
'O Redrigs, dear, hae ye tint your wut?
Are ye quite and clane gane wrang?
O spare my teapot! O spare my jug!
O spare, O spare my posset-mug!
And I'll let ye kiss, and I'll let ye hug,
Dear Redrigs, a' day lang.'
'Forgie, forgie me, my beauty bright!
Ye are my Nelly, my heart's delight;
I'll kiss and I'll hug ye day and night,
If alang wi' me you'll gang.'
'Fetch out my pillion, fetch out my cloak,
You'll heal my heart if my bowl you broke.'
These words, whilk she to her bridegroom spoke,
Are the endin' o' my sang.

I got this copy of his song since, else I could not have recollected it from that hearing; for I was too impatient to put the plan into execution for which I had come out, to attend even to this immortalizing of an ancestor.

I knew Ingram at once by his blue jacket, and the corkscrews which bobbed over each temple as he nodded and swayed his head to the flourishes of "the gaberlunzie man,[7]" (the measure which Halliday had chosen for his words;) so when the song was finished, and I had drank a health to Robin's muse, I stepped across to where he sat, and said I wished to speak with him alone. He put down his jug of punch, and followed me into my own room. I closed the door and told him, that as I understood him to be in the Channel trade, I applied to know if he could put me

[7] "The Gaberlunzie Man", Allan Ramsay's 1724 *Tea-table Miscellany*.

on any expeditious conveyance to the coast of France. "Why, sir," said he, "I could give you a cast myself in our own tight thing, the Saucy Sally, as far as Douglas or the Calf; and for the rest of the trip, why there's our consort, the Little Sweep, that will be thereabouts this week, would run you up, if it would lie in your way, as far as Guernsey, or, if need be, to Belle Isle." "Belle Isle!" repeated I, with a start; for the words of O'More to the priest came suddenly upon my recollection," Has any boat left this coast or that of Man for Belle Isle within the last fortnight?" "Not a keel, sir; there's ne'er a boat just now in the Channel that could do it but herself – they call her the Deil-sweep, sir, among the revenue sharks; for that's all that they could ever make of her. She is the only boat, sir, as I have said, and if so be you are a gentleman in distress, you will not be the only one that will have cause to trust to her – but, d—n it, (he muttered,) these women – well, what of that? – Mayn't I lend a hand to save a fine fellow for all that? – but harkye, brother, this is all in confidence."

"Your confidence shall not be abused," whispered I, hardly able to breathe for eager hope – the female passengers – the desire for exclusion – the only boat that fortnight, all confirmed me. "Mr O'More and I are friends; fear neither for him nor yourself; let me only get first onboard, and I can rough it all night on deck, as many a time I've done before: his daughter and her woman can have your cabin to themselves." It was a bold guess, but all right; he gaped at me for a minute in dumb astonishment; then closing one hand upon the earnest which I here slipped into it, drew the other across his eyes, as if to satisfy himself that he was not dreaming, and in a respectful tone informed me that they intended sailing on the next night from Cairn Castle shore. "We take the squire up off Island Magee, sir; he has been lying to on the look-out for us there for the last ten days; so that if you want to bear a hand in getting the young lady aboard, it will be all arranged to your liking."

During this conversation, my whole being underwent a wonderful change; from the collapsing sickness of bereavement, I felt my heart and limbs expand themselves under the delightful enlargement of this new spring of hope: I shook Ingram by the hand, led him back to the kitchen, and returned to the old man with a step so elated, and with such a kindling of animation over my whole appearance, that he exclaimed, in high glee, "Heard ye ever sic verses at Oxford, Willie? Odd! man, Rab Halliday is as good as a dozen o' Janet's possets for ye; I'll hae him here again to sing to ye the morn's e'en."

"He is a very pleasant fellow – a very pleasant fellow, indeed, sir; but I fear I shall not be able to enjoy his company to-morrow night, as I purpose taking my passage for the Isle of Man in Ingram's boat." – "Nonsense, Willie, nonsense; ye wadna make yoursell 'hail, billy[8], weel met,' wi' gallows-birds and vagabonds – though as for Paul himsell" – "My dear sir, you know I have my passport, and need not care for the reputation of my hired servants; besides, sir, you know how fond I am of excitement of all sorts, and the rogue really sings so well."

"That he does, Willie. Weel, weel – he that will to Cupar maun to Cupar!"[9] and so saying, he lifted up his candle and marched off the field without another blow.

Ingram and I started next evening about four o'clock, attended by little Davie, who was to bring back the horse I rode next day; Ingram, whose occupation lay as much on land as sea, was quite at home on his rough sheltie, which carried also a couple of little panniers at either side of the pommel, well-primed with samples

---

[8] billy = comrade, friend.
[9] 'He that will to Coupar maun to Coupar' is a Scottish proverb meaning "a wilful man must have his way".

of his contraband commodities. We arrived a little after nightfall in Larne, where we left Davie with the horses, while Ingram, having disposed of his pony, joined me on foot, and we set off by the now bright light of the moon along the hills for Cairn Castle. During the first three or four miles of our walk, he entertained me with abundance of songs echoed loud and long across the open mountain; but when we descended from it towards the sea, we both kept silence and a sharp look-out over the unequal and bleak country between. We now got among low clumpy hills and furzy gullies; and had to pick our steps through loose scattered lumps of rock, which were lying all round us white in the clear moonshine, like flocks of sheep upon the hill-side. The wind was off the shore, and we did not hear the noise of the water till, at the end of one ravine, we turned the angular jut of a low promontory, and beheld the image of the moon swinging in its still swell at our feet.

Ingram whistled, and was answered from the shore a little farther on; he stepped out a few paces in advance and led forward; presently I saw a light figure glide out of the shadow in front and approach us.

"Vell, mine Apostéle Paul, vat news of the Ephesiens?"

"All right, Munsher Martin, and here is another passenger."

He whispered something, and the little Frenchman touched his hat with an air; and expressed, in a compound of Norman-French, Manx, and English, the great pleasure he had in doing a service to the illustrious cavalier, the friend of liberty. Hearing a noise in front, I looked up and discerned the light spar of a mast peeping over an intervening barrier of rock; we wound round it, and on the other side found a cutter-rigged boat of about eighteen tons hauled close to the natural quay, with her mainsail set and flapping heavily in the night wind. Here we met another seaman. In ten minutes we were under way; the smooth groundswell running free and silent from our quarter, and the boat laying herself out with an easy speed, as she caught the breeze freshening over the lower coast. The Saucy Sally was a half-decked cutter, (built for a pleasure-boat in Guernsey,) and a tight thing, as Ingram had said. I did not go into the cabin, which occupied all the forecastle, but wrapping myself in my cloak, lay down along the stern-sheets, and feigned to be asleep, for I was so excited by the prospect of meeting Madeline, that I could no longer join in the conversation of the crew. In about half an hour I heard them say that we were in sight of Island Magee, and rising, beheld it dark over our weather-bows; I went forward and continued on the forecastle in feverish impatience as we neared it; the breeze stiffened as we opened Lame Lough, and the Saucy Sally tossed two or three sprinklings of cold spray over my shoulders, but I shook the water from my cloak and resumed my look-out. At last we were within a quarter of a mile of the coast, and a light appeared right opposite; we showed another and lay to; with a fluttering heart I awaited the approach of a boat; twice I fancied I saw it distinguish itself from the darkness of the coast, and twice I felt the blank recoil of disappointment; at last it did appear, dipping distinct from among the rocks and full of people; they neared us; my heart leapt at every jog of their oars in the loose thewels[10]; for I could now plainly discern two female figures, two boatmen, and a muffled man in the stern. All was now certain; they shot alongside, laid hold of the gunnel[11], and I heard O'More's voice call on Ingram to receive the lady; I could hardly conceal my agitation as she was lifted on deck, but had no power to advance; Nancy followed, and O'More himself leaped third on deck – the boat shoved off, the helmsman let the cutter's head away, the mainsail filled, and we stood out to sea.

---

[10]   thewel = A thole or tholepin – a holder attached to the gunwale of a boat that holds the oar in place and acts as a fulcrum for rowing.
[11]   gunnel = gunwale, the upper edge of a ship's or boat's side.

Here I was then, and would be for four-and-twenty hours at the least, by the side of her whom a little time before I would have given years of my life to have been near but for a minute; yet, with an unaccountable irresolution, I still delayed, nay, shrunk, from the long-sought interview. It was not till her father had gone into the little cabin to arrange it for her reception, and had closed the door between us, that I ventured from my hiding-place behind the foresail, and approached her where she stood gazing mournfully over the boat's side at the fast passing shores of her country. I whispered her name; she knew my voice at the first syllable, and turned in amazed delight; but the flush of pleasure which lit up her beautiful features as I clasped her hand, had hardly dawned ere it was chased by the rising paleness of alarm. I comforted her by assurances of eternal love, and vowed to follow her to the ends of the earth in despite of every human power. We stood alone; for two sailors were with O'More and the girl in the cabin, and the third, having lashed the tiller to, was fixing something forward. We stood alone I cannot guess how long – time is short, but the joy of those moments has been everlasting. We exchanged vows of mutual affection and constancy, and I had sealed our blessed compact with a kiss, witnessed only by the moon and stars, when the cabin-door opened, and her father stood before me. I held out my hand, and accosted him with the free confidence of a joyful heart. The severe light of the moon sharpened his strong features into startling expression, as he regarded me for a second with mingled astonishment and vexation. He did not seem to notice my offered hand, but saying something in a low, cold tone about the unexpected pleasure, turned to the steersman, and demanded fiercely why he had not abided by his agreement? The sailor, quailing before the authoritative tone and aspect of his really noble-looking questioner, began an exculpatory account of my having been brought thither by Ingram, to whom he referred.

Bold Paul was beginning with "Lookee, Squire, I'm master of

this same craft," when I interrupted him by requesting that he would take his messmates to the bows, and leave the helm with me, as I wished to explain the matter myself in private. He consigned his soul, in set terms, to the devil, if any other man than myself should be allowed to make a priest's palaver-box of the Saucy Sally, and sulkily retired, rolling his quid with indefatigable energy, and squirting jets of spittle half-mast high.

O'More almost pushed the reluctant Madeline into the cabin, closed the door, and addressed me. – "To what motive am I to attribute your presence here, Mr Macdonnell?"

"To one which I am proud to avow, the desire of being near the object of my sole affections, your lovely daughter; as well, sir, as from a hope that I may still be able to overcome those objections which you once expressed."

He pointed over the boat's side to the black piled precipices of the shore, as they stood like an iron wall looming along the weather-beam. – "Look there, sir; look at the Bloody Gobbins, and hear me – When a setting moon shall cease to fling the mourning of their shadows over the graves of *my* butchered ancestors, and when a rising sun shall cease to bare before abhorring Christendom" –

"Luff, sir, luff,"[12] cried Ingram, from the forecastle.

"Come aft yourself, Paul," I replied in despair and disgust.

O'More retired to the cabin bulkhead, and leaned against the door, without completing his broken vow. Ingram took the helm, and I sat down in silence. Paul saw our unpleasant situation, and ceasing to remember his own cause for ill-humour, strove to make us forget ours. He talked with a good deal of tact, but with little success, for the next half hour. O'More remained stern and black as the Gobbins themselves, now rapidly sinking astern, while the coast of Island Magee receded into the broad Lough of Belfast

---

[12] Luff = 'sail near the wind' in English. In Scots it also means 'to let well alone, steer clear of trouble'.

upon our quarter. The moon was still shining with unabated lustre, and we could plainly discern the bold outline of the hills beyond; while the coast of Down and the two Copelands lay glistening in grey obscure over our starboard bow. No sail was within sight; we had a stiff breeze with a swinging swell from the open bay; and as the cutter lay down and shewed the glimmer of the water's edge above her gunnel, the glee of the glorying sailor burst out in song.

> Haul away, haul away, down helm, I say;
>   Slacken sheets, let the good boat go –
> Give her room, give her room for a spanking boom;
>   For the wind comes on to blow –
>   (Haul away!)
>   For the wind comes on to blow,
> And the weather-beam is gathering gloom,
>   And the scud flies high and low.
> Lay her out, lay her out, till her timbers stout,
>   Like a wrestler's ribs, reply
> To the glee, to the glee of the bending tree,
>   And the crowded canvass high –
>   (Lay her out!)
>   And the crowded canvass high;
> Contending, to the water's shout,
>   With the champion of the sky.
> Carry on, carry on; reef none, boy, none;
>   Hang her out on a stretching sail:
> Gunnel in, gunnel in! for the race we'll win,
>   While the land-lubbers so pale –
>   (Carry on!)
>   While the land-lubbers so pale
> Are fumbling at their points, my son,
>   For fear of the coming gale!

All but O'More joined in the chorus of the last stanza, and the bold burst of harmony was swept across the water like a defiance to the eastern gale. Our challenge was accepted. "Howsomever," said Ingram, after a pause, and running his glistening eye along the horizon, "as we are not running a race, there will be no harm in taking in a handful or two of our cloth tins morning; for the wind is chopping round to the north, and I wouldn't wonder to hear Sculmarten's breakers under our lee before sunrise."

"And a black spell we will have till then, for when the moon goes down you may stop your fingers in your eyes for starlight," observed the other sailor, as he began to slacken down the peak halliards; while they brought the boat up and took in one reef in the mainsail; but the word was still "helm a larboard," and the boat's head had followed the wind round a whole quarter of the compass within the next ten minutes. We went off before the breeze, but it continued veering round for the next hour; so that when we got fairly into the Channel, the predictions of the seamen were completely fulfilled; for the moon had set, the wind was from the east, and a hurrying drift had covered all the sky.

We stood for the north of Man; but the cross sea, produced by the shifting of the wind, which was fast rising to a gale, buffeted us with such contrary shocks, thai after beating through it almost till the break of day, we gave up the hope of making Nesshead, and, altering our course, took in another reef, and ran for the Calf.

But the gale continued to increase; we pitched and plunged to no purpose; the boat was going bows in at every dip, and the straining of her timbers as she stooped out to every stretch, told plainly that we must either have started planks or an altered course again. The sailors, after some consultation, agreed on putting about; and, for reasons best known to themselves, pitched upon Strangford Lough as their harbour of refuge. Accordingly we altered our course once more, and went off before the wind. Day broke as we were still toiling ten miles from the coast of Down.

The grey dawn shewed a black pile of clouds overhead, gathering bulk from rugged masses which were driving close and rapid from the east. By degrees the coast became distinct from the lowering sky; and at last the sun rose lurid and large above the weltering waters. It was ebb tide, and I represented that Strangford bar at such a time was peculiarly dangerous in an eastern gale; nevertheless the old sailor who was now at the helm insisted on standing for it. When we were yet a mile distant, I could distinguish the white horses running high through the black trembling strait, and hear the tumult of the breakers over the dashing of our own bows. Escape was impossible; we could never beat to sea in the teeth of such a gale; over the bar we must go, or founder. We took in the last reef, hauled down our jib, and, with ominous faces, saw ourselves in ten minutes more among the cross seas and breakers.

The waters of a wide estuary running six miles an hour, and meeting the long roll of the Channel, might well have been expected to produce a dangerous swell; but a spring-tide combining with a gale of wind, had raised them at flood to an extraordinary height, and the violence of their discharge exceeded our anticipations accordingly. We had hardly encountered the first two or three breakers, when Ingram was staggered from the forecastle by the buffet of a counter sea, which struck us forward just as the regular swell caught us astern; the boat heeled almost on her beam ends, and he fell over the cabin door into the hold; the man at the helm was preparing for the tack as he saw his messmate's danger, and started forward to save him: he was too late; the poor fellow pitched upon his head and shoulders among the ballast; at the same instant the mainsail caught the wind, the boom swung across, and striking the helmsman on the back of the neck, swept him half overboard, where he lay doubled across the gunnel, with his arms and head dragging through the water, till I hauled him in. He was stunned and nearly scalped by the blow. Ingram lay moaning and motionless; the boat was at the mercy of the elements, while I stretched the poor fellows side by side at our feet. I had now to take the helm, for the little Frenchman was totally ignorant of the coast; he continued to hand the main-sheet; and O'More, who all night long had been sitting in silence against the cabin bulkhead, leaped manfully upon the forecastle and stood by the tackle there. We had now to put the boat upon the other tack, for the tide made it impossible to run before the wind. O'More belayed his sheet, and, as the cutter lay down again, folded his arms and leaned back on the weather bulwark, balancing himself with his feet against the skylight.

The jabble around us was like the seething of a caldron; for the waves boiled up all at once, and ran in all directions. I was distracted by their universal assault, and did not observe the heaviest and most formidable of all, till it was almost down upon our broadside. I put the helm hard down, and shouted with all my might to O'More – "Stand by for a sea, sir, lay hold, lay hold." It was too late. I could just prevent our being swamped, by withdrawing our quarter from the shock, when it struck us on the weather-bows, where he stood: it did not break. Our hull was too small an obstacle: it swept over the forecastle as the stream leaps a pebble, stove in the bulwark, lifted him right up, and launched him on his back, with his feet against the foresail: the foresail stood the shock a moment, and he grappled to it, while we were swept on in the rush, like a sparrow in the clutches of a hawk; but the weight of water bore all before it—the sheets were torn from the deck, the sail flapped up above the water, and I saw him tossed from its edge over the lee-bow. The mainsail hid him for a moment; he reappeared, sweeping astern at the rate of fifteen knots an hour. He was striking out, and crying for a rope; there was no rope at hand, and all the loose spars had been stowed away: He could not be saved. I have said that the sun had just risen: between us and the east his rays shone through the tops of the higher waves with a pale and livid light; as O'More drifted into these, his whole agonized figure rose for a moment dusk in the transparent water, then disappeared in the hollow beyond; but at our next plunge I saw him heaved up again, struggling dim amid the green gloom of an overwhelming sea. An agonizing cry behind me made me turn my head. "O save him, save him! turn the boat, and save him! O William, as you love me, save my father!" It was Madeline, frantic for grief, stumbling over, and unconsciously treading on the wounded men, as she rushed from the cabin, and cast herself upon her knees before me. I raised my eyes to heaven, praying for support; and though the clouds rolled, and the gale swept between, strength was surely sent me from above; for what save heavenly help could have subdued that fierce despair, which, at the first sight of the complicated agonies around, had prompted me to abandon hope, blaspheme, and die? I raised her gently but firmly in my arms; drew her, still struggling and screaming wild entreaties, to my breast, and not daring to trust myself with a single look at her imploring eyes, fixed my own upon the course we had to run, and never swerved from my severe determination, till the convulsive sobs had ceased to shake her breast upon mine, and I had felt the warm gush of her relieving tears instead; then my stern purpose melted, and, bending over the desolate girl, I murmured, "Weep no more, my Madeline, for, by the blessing of God, I will be a father and a brother to you yet!" Blessed be he who heard my holy vow! – when I looked up again we were in the smooth water.

Drenched, numbed, and dripping all with the cold spray, one borne senseless and bloody in his mess-mate's arms, we climbed the quay of Strangford: the threatened tempest was bursting in rain and thunder; but our miserable plight had attracted a sympathizing crowd. No question was asked of who? or whence? by a generous people, to wounded and wearied men and helpless women; till there pressed through the ring of bystanders a tall fellow, with a strong expression of debasement and desperate impudence upon his face, that seemed to say, "Infamy, you have done your worst." He demanded our names and passports, and arrested us all in the king's name, almost in the same breath. I struck him in the face with my fist, and kicked him into the kennel. No one attempted to lift him; but he scrambled to his feet, with denunciations of horrible revenge. He was hustled about by the crowd till he lost temper, and struck one of them. He had now rather too much work upon his hands to admit of a too close attention to us: three or four persons stepped forward and offered us protection.

Ingram and the other wounded sailor were taken off, along with the Frenchman, by some of their own associates; while a respectable and benevolent looking man addressed me, "I am a Protestant, sir, and an Orangeman; but put these ladies under my protection, and you will not repent your confidence; for, next to the Pope, I love to defeat an informer;" and he pointed with a smile to our arrester, who was just measuring his length upon the pavement.

"Is his name Macdonnell?" asked I.

"The same, sir," he replied; "but come away with me before he gets out of my Thomas's hands, and I will put your friends out of the reach of his."

I shall never be able to repay the obligation I owe to this good man, who received Miss O'More, with her attendant, into the bosom of his family, till I had arranged her journey to the house of a female relative, whence, after a decent period of mourning, our marriage permitted me to bear her to my own.

The Ornithologist

Thomas Stott (1805)

[**Editor's note:** This poem appeared in the *Belfast Commercial Chronicle* in 1805, and has never been republished before now. It is one of several poems in Ulster-Scots penned for Belfast newspapers by Thomas Stott (1755-1829), a County Down poet better known by his pseudonym 'Hafiz', who is usually associated with rarefied Spenserian verse.]

> I chanc'd to tak a random ring.
> Amang the haughs whare birdies sing
>   Their varied sang;
> Some perching, some upo' the wing,
>   A tunefu' thrang:
>
> An' the mingl'd concert raise
> Frae blooming dells an' echoing braes,
> To nature's Queen, in beauty's praise.
>   On ev'ry han',
> My Muse thought she some o' the lays
>   Cou'd understan'.
>
> The Mavis, on the ash-crown'd hill,
> Garbled a sprightly French tune still;
> The Blackbird, near the murm'ring rill,
>   Italian saft;
> The Lavrock, wi' her pipe sae shrill,
>   Braid Scotch, alaft.

The Lintwhite, on the chirry-tree.
In Irish chaunted her short glee;
The Gowd-spink, fine as fine cou'd be,
    A Spanish strain
But hamely Robin, bauld an' free,
    In English plain.

The wee Wren, cocktail'd, frae the hedge,
(whase note might set ane's teeth on edge;)
The Wullie-wagtail the sedge,
    Or burnie's brink;
The Whin-chat, on the rocks stey ledge,
    Thrumm'd Welsh, I think.

The Kaes an' Corbies, (a black clutch)
Screigh'd in low German, or high Dutch,
But I'se nae venture to avouch
    Whilk o' the twa,
Yet I'm quite certain o' this much—
    They clos'd wi'—*caw*.

Pianets, wha high stations seek,
To sun themsels, an' feathers sleek,
Tun'd their learn'd eulogies in Greek,
    Which I'm but flat in;
The Cushat, Cuckoo, an' Corncreak.
    Sang their's in Latin.

But tak the music a' thegither,
Join'd wi' the season, scene, an' weather,
Whether I scanned it right, or whether
    'Twas magic wrought,
My Muse an' I felt joy that neither
    Has yet forgot.
                    — HAFIZ.

[BIRD-NAMES: **Mavis** = song thrush; **Lavrock** = skylark; **Lintwhite** = linnet; **Gowd-spink** = goldfinch; **Wullie-wagtail** = pied wagtail; **Kaes an' Corbies** = jackdaws and ravens / rooks; **Pianets** = magpies; **Cushat** = woodpigeon.]

Ulster-Scots bird names: notes towards a trial list[1]

John Erskine

The subtitle to this article, 'notes towards a trial list', might seem to the reader somewhat cautious. It is. And it's meant to be.

This article was first intended to be a short exploration of the bird names used by Thomas Given in his poetry. However, very few of these turned out to be actually Scots — the exceptions are Bluebonnet, Craw, Mavis, Whaup, Whun Gray, Yellow Yorling and Yoit — because Given, even in those of his poems written in Ulster-Scots, tends to use standard English bird names. Shortly after the examination of Given, the revised edition of Robin Jackson's splendid *A guide to Scots bird names* (Ptarmigan Press, 2013) was published and it revived an old interest.

Purpose of the list

Perhaps it would be easier to start by saying what this article is not. First of all, it is not a definitive list of Ulster-Scots bird names. Furthermore, it is not the work of an ornithologist but of a casual and often perplexed back-garden birdwatcher. And it is not the result of extensive or first-hand linguistic fieldwork. It's a work of synthesis, and it relies heavily on transcribed and re-transcribed

---

[1] *This article is dedicated to the memory and friendship of Julian Greenwood, colleague and ornithologist, whose knowledge and expertise would have improved it immeasurably.*

lists. And it does not set out to give *the* Ulster-Scots name for a particular bird, though standardization certainly has its place. Is there an Ulster-Scots name for a Yellowhammer, for example? No. There isn't. There are about thirty of them. And many a local name, such as Blackcap (and its spelling variants), can apply to several different species.

So what is this list intended to be? If we already have John Braidwood's authoritative and exhaustive work on local bird names in Ulster published in *Ulster Folklife*, and if we have the *Concise Ulster Dictionary*, and if we have also the continuing lexicographical work of the Language Society developed by Philip Robinson, what is the point of this list? Well, it is an attempt to work towards a listing of bird names specifically in Ulster-Scots rather than more broadly in Ulster dialect. But where one ends and the other begins, and where they overlap, is part of the process of discovery.

Regional, local, English or Ulster-Scots?

With the clear and outstanding exception of James Fenton's work, the sources for this listing have been many of those local and regional lists, some of them nineteenth-century, which were used by John Braidwood in his work on local bird names in Ulster: those lists are not, in themselves, intended to be Ulster-Scots lists. However, an attempt has been made here to concentrate on those lists emanating from areas where the presence of Ulster-Scots language is or was strong. This article has also greatly benefited from the generous contribution by Philip Robinson of many of those bird names he has found in his lexicographical work on Ulster-Scots literature. And, of course, this article becomes immediately out-of-date as more sources come to hand.

It could be argued, too, that many of the names found here are simply English and not Ulster-Scots names at all. What is specifically Ulster-Scots about, for example, Bald Coot, Black

Duck (Common Scoter) and Long-necked Heron? Apparently
nothing. However, it seems we should allow for the existence of
parallel Ulster-Scots spellings and for the fact that the compilers
of lists may have silently (and unwittingly) 'corrected' Ulster-Scots
names in the compilation of their lists: for example, from Beld
Cuit (Jackson), Black Deuk (Jackson) and Lang-neckit Hern (Fenton). And does Bog Sparrow (Reed Bunting), for one, not seem
more likely to have started out as Boag Sparra?

Comparison with Jackson's valuable work (it contains both
Scots-to-English and English-to-Scots lists) has been fascinating.
It has revealed both overlap and also clear differences with Scots.
For example, the Scots and Ulster-Scots lists of names for Brent
Goose and for Red-breasted Merganser do not overlap at all. This
perhaps also suggests considerable lexical loss in Ulster. There are
also, perhaps unsurprisingly, a greater number of names in Scots.

Terminology and identification

There are indeed many and obvious weaknesses in this list. The
inclusion of many, often standard, names from, for example, William Thompson's work may simply have had the result of diluting
the number of Ulster-Scots terms listed here. However, Thompson's work is both fascinating and indispensable in assessing early
nineteenth-century lists. Clearly too, some compilers have simply
mis-identified certain birds. And the compiler of this list must
admit to probable mis-attribution also, not least for the 'Greys'
(Hedge, Nettley, Red, Rosy, Thorn and Whin). Furthermore, the
recording here of numerous minimal variants in spelling — vari-
ations on "Peewit" or "Lang-neckit Hern," for example — may
seem an extravagance, especially where some of the spellings are
likely to have been in themselves randomly idiosyncratic; and,
indeed, where transcription for this article may itself have unwittingly introduced yet more variation. And there are further lists
which could and perhaps should have been included. However, a

decision had to be made to issue a list for consultation before the whole project simply collapsed under its own weight.

The scientific names used for birds also keep changing. The scientific names adopted here are the most current ones, yet they often differ considerably from those used in the sources consulted, particularly the earlier sources. And the English names given here are the common standard names, the names that most people recognize. Where possible the names of birds are filed alphabetically in inverted form (as in the index to a bird book): e.g. 'Hooded Crow' is listed as 'Crow, Hooded'. This may make finding a specific bird easy, and it collocates some birds from the same family, but it also scatters others — for example in the cases of thrushes and crows — throughout the list. Both the English and scientific names are based on the Northern Ireland Birdwatchers' Association list.

Consulting the older standard texts on Irish ornithology in the course of this compilation has proved fascinating and has revealed much about the fluctuation in the populations of certain species. Indeed, William Thompson's observations, written over one hundred and fifty years ago, on the decline in the numbers of various species, though loss of habitat and environmental damage — although he does not use those precise terms — read as if they come from a report on bird conservation published only yesterday. And it comes as something of a surprise too that, in the days before photography and the general use of binoculars and telescopes, shooting birds, not least by bird enthusiasts, was the surest way to identify them. What's hit is history, what's missed is mystery, as the saying has it. Robert Patterson, just over a century ago, after recording the local shooting of a Rough-legged Buzzard, a Grey Phalarope, a Hawfinch, a Hoopoe and a Marsh Harrier, was driven to conclude: "It would appear that any uncommon bird has a poor chance of surviving its visit to the over-populated 'Black North'."

Mapping the names with your help

Yet, despite all the caveats, making a start on this list, at the time, seemed like a useful thing to do. So here it is, for what it is worth: incomplete, unwieldy and imperfect. The compiler would very much welcome comments, corrections and additions to the list. It would be greatly appreciated if readers would submit bird names, both new names and names that confirm those listed here, along with the location (and the BT number of the postcode for that location) in which the name is or was used. This will assist in the mapping of terminology, will develop the database and will render it more useful. Anyway, see what you make of it.

. . . .

When he had presented his list of bird names to the *Northern Whig* in 1922, "H. G. McW" concluded his article thus: "Most of the other birds are known by their right name or have none at all." If only it were that simple …

. . . .

Ulster-Scots bird names

General, generic and collective names

Auks	Fry birds (FS)
Bird of prey, Large	Glead, Kite (WT)
Crow (generic?)	Corbie (JM); Cra (JF); Craw (GD) (TG) (JM) (ST)
Duck	Duke (WP)
Duck, farmyard	Wheetie (WP)
Finch	Flinch (WP)
Fledglings	Scaldies (GM)
Godwit	Stone-plover (WH)
	Yarwhelp, Yarwhip (WH) (WP)
Goose, Greylag/Bean/ White-fronted	? Harrow Goose (WH) (WT)
Grebes	(2 species) Divers (HM)
Guillemot	Cutty (CD)
	Willock (EA) (CS)
Gull	Gull (TG)
	Seagull (HM)
Hawk	Hak (JF)
Hedge song bird	Chitterareery(JM)
Large bird	Barge (WP)
	Harrow goose (WH) (WP)
Martins	Swallows (HM)
Owl	Ool (JF); Ule (XG)
Plover	Pliver (JF)
Puffin	Cutty (CD)
Razorbill	Cutty (CD)
	Willock (EA) (CS)
Swimming bird, small	Whitterick (WP) (see also Little Grebe)
Tern	Fish Swallow (XG); Pier (FS) Pirr (GM)

	(RP); Pirre-maw (WP); Purr (RP); Purre (WP); Pyrmaw (WP); Sea Swallow (EA) (DD) (WG) (HM); Skirr (WP)
Thrush (generic?)	Mavis (WP); Mavish (JM); Thrush (TG)
Titmouse	(3 species) Bluebonnets (HM) Tittymouse (GM)
Waders, small	Sandpipers (e.g. Ringed Plover, Knot, Turnstone, Dunlin) (XG) Sandy Larks (e.g. Dunlin, Sanderling, Sandpiper etc.) (SH) Sanny-larks (WG)
Wagtails	(2 species) Willie Wagtails (HM)
Waterfowl	Braid-fit (RH)

Specific birds

Auk, Great		
(*extinct*)	*Pinguinus impennis*	Garefowl (EA)
		Great Auk (WT)
		Pinguin (GS)
Bittern	*Botaurus stellaris*	Bittern (JD) (WH)
		Bittour (WH)
		Bog Bluiter (*per LS*)
Blackbird	*Turdus merula*	Black Bird (SM)
		Black-bird (WH)
		Blackbird (TG) (SM) (GS) (TS) (WT)
		Blakburd (JF)
		Bleckburd (JF)
		Merle (EA)
Blackcap	*Sylvia atricapilla*	Black-cap (GS) (WT)
		Blakkep (JF)
		Bleckkep (JF)
Brambling	*Fringilla montifringilla*	Brammle finch (JF)
Bullfinch	*Pyrrhula pyrrhula*	Bul-flinch (WG)
		Bullfinch (SM) (GS) (WT)
		Bullie (*per*)
Bunting,		
Corn	*Emberiza calandra*	Briar Bunting (WP) (CS)
		Briar-Bunting (WT)
		Bunting (SM) (GS)
		Bunting Lark (NF)
		Buntling (SM)
		Chitteraragh
		Common bunting (JC) (WT)
		Corn Bunting (JC)
		Corn-Bunting (WT)
		Thistle Cock (NF)
		Thristle Cock (JC) (WP)

Bunting, Reed	*Emberiza schoeniclus*	Black Cap (DD)
		Blackcap (SH)
		Black Head (JC) (WG) (SM)
		Black-head (PW)
		Blackhead (NF)
		Bog Sparrow (DD)
		Ringrasher (JF)
		Rush Sparrow (NF) (JC)
		Water Sparrow (HM)
Bunting, Snow	*Plectrophenax nivalis*	Snow Bird (DD)
		Snow Bunting (SM)
		Snow Flake (WG)
Buzzard	*Buteo buteo*	*Bussard (RH)*
		Buzzard (WT) (HW)
		Glead (WT)
		Kite (WT)
Chaffinch	*Fringilla coelebs*	Chaffie (*per*)
		Chaffinch (GS) (WT)
		Twink (WG)
Chiffchaff	*Phylloscopus collybita*	Chiff-chaff (WT)
		Lesser Pettychaps (WT)
		White Wran (TM)
Chough	*Pyrrhocorax pyrrhocorax*	Chough (SM) (WT)
		Cornish chough (JD) (WH) (WT)
		Red-legged Crow (SH) (WT)
		Red-legged Jackdaw (SM) (WT)
Coot	*Fulica atra*	Bald Coot (NF) (WG) (SM) (WT)
		Common Coot (WT)
		Coot (JD) (GS)
		Drink-a-penny (SM) (WP)
		Waterhen (TM)

Cormorant	*Phalacrocorax carbo*	Black Diver (WG)
		Black Scart (WP)
		Common Cormorant (WT)
		Cormoral (WP)
		Cormorant (SM) (GS)
		Corvorant (SM) (WP)
		Diver (XG) (SH)
		Divie Duck (HM)
		Great Cormorant (WT)
		Karbee (WG)
		Scart (DD) (SH) (GM) (HM) (LM) (SM) (WP) (CS)
		Skarf (JC) (JF) (FS)
		Skart (EA) (JC) (CD) (SM) (WP) (WT)
		Wool Cottar (WP)
		Wully-dooker (JMy)
Corncrake	*Crex crex*	Coarncrake (JF)
		Coarncrek (JF)
		Corn Craik (SM)
		Corn-creak (WH)
		Corncreak (TS)
		Corncraik (GD) (JM)
		Corncrake (TG) (WT)
		Crake (JF)
		Crek (JF)
		Land Rail (GD) (JM) (SM)
		Land-rail (WT)
		Rail (JD) (WH) (GS)
Crake, Spotted	*Porzana porzana*	Spotted Crake (WT)
		Spotted Rail (WT)
		Spotted water-hen (SM) (GS)
Crossbill, Common	*Loxia curvirostra*	Cross-bill (WH) (SM)
		Crossbill (WT)

		Gross-beak (JD)
		Sheld-apple (WH)
Crow, Carrion	*Corvus corone*	Carren Crow (EA)
		Carrion Crow (WT)
		Crow (WT)
Crow, Hooded	*Corvus cornix*	Corbie (JF) (?TS)
		Corby (WP)
		Grey Crow (EA) (WG) (XG) (SH) (SM) (WT)
		Hooded Crow (SM) (WT)
		Hoodie (JF)
		Hoody Crow (WG)
		Royston Crow (EA)
Cuckoo	*Cuculus canorus*	Cuckoo (TG) (SM) (ST) (TS)
		Cuckow (GS)
		Goak (WK) (WP)
		Gouk (WP)
		Gowk (GD) (JF) (JM) (WT)
Curlew	*Numenius arquata*	Common Curlew (SM)
		Courliew (WG)
		Curleu (WH)
		Curlew (JD) (JF) (GS) (WT)
		Whaap (CD) (HM) (RP) (WT)
		Whap (JF) (TM)
		Whaup (DD) (TG) (WG) (SH) (GM) (LM) (RP) (WP) (FS)
Dipper	*Cinclus cinclus*	Dipper (WT)
		Ducker (WG)
		Water Blackbird (JC) (WT)
		Water-Crow (NF)
		Water Ouzel (JD) (NF) (WH) (WT)
		Water-creak (WH)
		Water-ouzel (SM)

Water Ousel (NF)
Water-hen (SM)
Waterhen (SM)

Diver, Great Northern	*Gavia immer*	Allan Hawk (RP) (WP) Arran Auk (RP) Great Northern Diver (WT) Holland Hawk (WP) Imber Diver (WT) Northern Diver (SM)
Diver, Red -throated	*Gavia stellata*	Allan Hawk (CD) (RP) (WP) Allan-Hawk (SM) Arran-Ake (SM) Burrian (WP) Diving Widgeon (DD) First Speckled Diver (WT) Hollan Hawk (SK) Holland/Allan Hawk (WP) Loon (SM) Red-throated Diver (WT) Second Speckled Diver (WT) Speckled Diver (SM) (WT)
Dove, Rock (*see also* Pigeon, Feral)	*Columba livia*	Blue Rock (XG) ? Blue Rock Pigeon (JC) ? Pigeon (GS) Rock Lark (DD) (WG) Rock Pigeon (XG) Rock-Dove (WT) Rock-Pigeon (TW)
Dunlin	*Calidris alpina*	Pir (SM) Purr (SM) Purre (RP) (SM) (WT) ? Sea Lark (CS) Sandlark (DD) (RP); (winter) (CD)

		Sandlark of the Shore (WT)
		Stint (SM)
Dunnock	*Prunella modularis*	Blue Wran (WG)
		Dunnock (WT)
		Grey Robin (CD)
		Hedge Sparrow (WG) (HM) (SM) (GS)
		Hedge-Accentor (WT)
		Hedge-Sparrow (WT)
		Hedge-Warbler (WT)
		Whin Sparrow (CD) (HM)
Eagle, Golden	*Aquila chrysaetos*	Golden Eagle (JD) (GS) (WT)
Eagle, White-tailed	*Haliaeetus albicilla*	Sea-eagle (JD) (GS) (WT)
		White-tailed Eagle (GS) (WT)
Fieldfare	*Turdus pilaris*	Big Felt (WT)
		Blue Felt (JC) (JF) (NF)
		Blue Pigeon (WT)
		Felt (DD) (NF) (WG) (XG) (HM)
		Felt Thrush (NF)
		Fieldfare (SM) (GS) (WT)
		Large Blue Felt (WP)
		Phelt (SM)
		Pigeon (SM)
Fulmar	*Fulmarus glacialis*	New Gull (CD)
Gannet	*Morus bassanus*	Bass Goose (WH)
		Gannet (SM)
		Scout (WH)
		Solan goose (RP) (WT)
		Soland Goose (WH)
Godwit, Bar-tailed	*Limosa lapponica*	Barge (WH)
		Godwit (WH)
		Spool Whaup (LM)

LIMOSA rufa *Rostrothe Uferschnepfe*

1 Sommerkl. 2 Winterkl. 3 Jugendkl.

Spoolwhap (Bar-tailed Godwit)

Gowdspink (Goldfinch)

		Spoolwhap (JMy)
		Stone-plover (WH)
		Yarwhelp (WH) (CS)
		Yarwhip (WH) (CS)
Godwit,		
Black-tailed	*Limosa limosa*	Barge (WH)
		Yarwhelp (WH)
		Yarwip (WH)
Goldcrest	*Regulus regulus*	Gold-crested Regulus (WT)
		Gold-crested Wren (WT)
		Golden Crested Wren (SM)
		Golden-crested Wren (NF) (GS)
		Half Moon (JC) (NF)
		Half-moons (CD)
		Pope's Eye (NF)
		Siskin (HM)
Goldeneye	*Bucephala clangula*	Golden Eye (SM)
		Golden-eye Duck (WT)
		Morillon (♀, young ♂, WT)
		Whiteside (WP)
Goldfinch	*Carduelis carduelis*	Goldfinch (SM) (GS) (WT)
		Goldspink (JC) (WT)
		Goldie (GM)
		Gooldie (JF) (GM) (JM) (*per*)
		Gooldpink (JM) [sic]
		Goldspring (JC) (WG) (WP)
		Gowd-spink (TS)
		Gowdspink (RH) (ST)
		Spink (NF) (JC)
Goosander	*Mergus merganser*	? Goosander (SM)
		Dun diver (♀, young ♂) (WT)
Goose,		
Barnacle	*Branta leucopsis*	Bernacle (WT)
		Land barnacle (WH)
		White-faced Barnacle (CD)
		White-faced Bernacle (WT)

Goose, Brent	*Branta bernicla*	Barnacle (EA) (CD) (WG) (WH) (HM) (SM) (RP)
		Bernacle (XG)
		Brent Goose (SM)
		Wild Goose (HM)
Goose, Greylag	*Anser anser*	? Wild Goose (JD) (SM)
Grebe, Great Crested	*Podiceps cristatus*	Big Diver (JC)
		Crested Grebe (WT)
		Great-crested Grebe (WT)
		? Horn Ouzel (WH) (WP)
		? Molrooken (CS) (WP)
		Tippet grebe (WT)
Grebe, Little	*Tachybaptus ruficollis*	Blackchin Grebe (WT)
		Dab Chick (WG)
		Dabchick (EA) (WT)
		Dam Puddin (EA)
		Drink-a-penny (WP)
		Little Grebe (SM) (WT)
		Penny Bird (SM) (WP) (CS)
		Tam Pudden (JC) (CS)
		Tam Puddin (EA)
		Tam Puddins Diver (NF)
		Tamwhinny (SH)
		Tom Pudden (WP)
		Tom Puddin (CS)
		Wee Diver (WG)
		Whitterick (WP)
		Willie Hawkie (WP) (CS)
Greenfinch	*Carduelis chloris*	Green finch (GS)
		Greenfinch (WT)
		Green Linnet (DD) (SH) (HM) (SM) (WT)
		Greenlinnet (JC)
Grouse, Red	*Lagopus lagopus scotica*	Grous (GS)

Tam Puddin (Little Grebe)

Coulterneb (Puffin)

		Grouse (SM)
		Moorcock (SM)
		Moor Hen (SH) (WG)
		Red Game (WT)
		Red grouse (WT)
Guillemot	*Uria aalge*	Common guillemot (WT)
		Cutty (RP) (WP)
		Drink-a-penny (LM)
		Foolish Guillemot (WT)
		Puffin (JC) (WG) (XG) (RP)
		Sea Pigeon (DD)
Guillemot,		
Black	*Cepphus grylle*	Black Guillemot (SM)
		Black Puffin (WG)
		Sea Pigeon (EA) (CS)
Gull,		
Black-headed	*Chroiocephalus ridibundus*	Black Headed Gull (SM)
		Common Gull (CD)
		Permas (DD)
		Pewit Gull (SM)
		Pirre (WT)
		Pirre-maw (WT)
		Purre (WP)
		Red-legged Gull (WT)
Gull,		
Common	*Larus canus*	Common Gull (WT)
		Gull (GS)
Gull, Great Black -backed	*Larus marinus*	Black Backed Gull (SM)
		Saddleback (FS)
Gull, Lesser Black -backed	*Larus fuscus*	(?) Herring Gull (SM) (GS)
		Lesser Black-backed Gull (WT)

Harrier, Hen	*Circus cyaneus*	Hen Harrier (WT)
		Ringtail (WT)
		White Hawk (WT)
Harrier, Marsh		*Circus aeruginosus* Marsh Harrier (WT)
		Moor Buzzard (SM) (WT)
Heron, Grey	*Ardea cinerea*	Cran (DD) (NF)
		Crane (CD) (NF) (WG) (SH) (WT)
		Cranny (HM) (LM)
		Crit-the-cran (LM)
		Hern (WG)
		Hern Cran (NF)
		Herncran/crane (WP)
		Heron (JD) (GS) (WT)
		Heron Cran (FS) (NF)
		Heron-cran (HM)
		Heron Crane (JC)
		Jinny (FS)
		Lang-necked hern (WG)
		Lang-necked kerin (WG)
		Lang-neckit hern (JF)
		Long Necked Heron (SM) (WT)
		Long-necked hern (DD)
		Long-necked Heron (TM)
Hoopoe	*Upupa epops*	Hoopoe (SM) (WT)
Jackdaw	*Corvus monedula*	Crow (DD) (XG)
		Daw (EA) (JC) (DH)
		Jackdaw (SM) (GS) (WT)
		Jakeda (*per KMcL*)
		Jeckda (JF)
		Kae (TS) (ST)
		Kay (ST)
Jay	*Garrulus glandarius*	Jay (JD) (WT)
Kestrel	*Falco tinnunculus*	Hawk (JC)

		Kestrel (WT)
		Kestril (SM)
		Peep Hawk (WP)
		Peepe Hawk (SM)
		Wind Hover (SM)
		Wind-hover (WT)
		Windhover (DD) (SH)
Kingfisher	*Alcedo atthis*	King-fisher (JD) (GS)
		Kingfisher (WT)
		King's fisher (WH) (SM)
		Water Owl (WG)
Kite, Red	*Milvus milvus*	Gled (WP)
		Kite (GS) (WT)
Kittiwake	*Rissa tridactyla*	Chitty-winke (DD)
		Kittiwake (SM) (WT)
		Tarrock (SM)
Knot	*Calidris canutus*	Ash-coloured Sandpiper (WT)
		Dunne (WP) (CS)
		Grey Plover (CD)
Lapwing	*Vanellus vanellus*	Bastard Plover (WH) (SM)
		Green Plover (WG) (SM) (WT) (NF)
		Green Plover Lapwing (JD)
		Lapwing (WH) (WG) (SM) (GS) (WT)
		Peeweep (JF) (TM)
		Peesweep (DD) (JF) (WP)
		Peesweet (WK)
		Peeweet (WP)
		Peewheep (WG)
		Peewheat (JC)
		Peewheet (JM)
		Peewit (NF) (WG) (HM) (RP) (WT)
		Pewit (JD) (SM)
		Tewet (WH)

Linnet	*Carduelis cannabina*	Common Linnet (WT)
		Greater Redpole (WT)
		Gray/Grey (XG) (WG) (SH) (HM) (JO) (WP)
		Grey Linnet (GM) (SM) (WT)
		Hedge Grey (WP)
		Linnet (ST)
		Lint-white (WP)
		Lintwhite (TS)
		Lintie (DD) (JF)
		Linty (GM) (WP)
		Rosy-finch ♂ (JF)
		Thorn Grey (WP)
		Whin Grey (JC) (DD) (GM) (CS) (TM)
		Whin-gray (WT)
		Whun Gray (TG)
		Whunny-grey (JF)
Magpie	*Pica pica*	Magpie (JF) (SM) (WT)
		Magpye (GS)
		Megpie (JF)
		Pianet (TS)
		Pie (RH)
		Piet (FB) (WG)
		Piot (WK)
		Pye (EA)
		Pyet (JF)
		Pyot (WP)
Mallard	*Anas platyrhynchos*	? Flapper (JM)
		Mallard (SM) (GS) (WT)
		Wild Duck (JD) (HM) (SM) (RP) (WT)
Martin, House	*Delichon urbicum*	Martin (SM) (GS)
		House-Martin (WT)
		Swallow (TM)

		White Rumped Martin (SM)
Martin, Sand	*Riparia riparia*	Sand Martin (SM)
		Sand Swallow (WG)
		Sand-martin (GS)
		Sand-Martin (WT)
		Swallow (TM)
Merganser,		
Red-breasted	*Mergus serrator*	Bar Duck (NF)
		Bar-drake (WP)
		Bar-duck (WP)
		Herring Scale (WG)
		Less diver (GS)
		Red-breasted Merganser (WT)
		Saw-bill (EA)
		Scale Duck (EA) (LM) (CS) (WT)
		Scaledrake (FS)
		Scameler (EA)
		Scamler (EA)
		Scammler (CD)
		Scemler (JMy)
		Skiel Duck (JC)
		Spear Wigeon (EA) (NF)
Moorhen	*Gallinula chloropus*	Common Gallinule (WT)
		Common Waterhen (WT)
		Moorhen (WT)
		Water Hen (JC)
		Water-hen (JD) (NF) (GS)
		Waterhen (SH) (RP)
		Watterhen (JF)
Nightjar	*Caprimulgus europaeus*	Reeler (CD)
Ouzel, Ring	*Turdus torquatus*	Ring Ouzel (WH)
		? Rock Ouzel (♀WH)
Owl, Barn	*Tyto alba*	Barn Owl (WT)
		White ool (JF) (WG)
		White Owl (JC) (SH) (GS) (WT)

Owl,
Long-eared   *Asio otus*   Brown Owl (JC)
                                  Common Owl (SM)
                                  Long-eared owl (WT)
                                  Ool (WG)
                                  Owl (SH)
Oystercatcher *Haematopus ostralegus* Limpet Picker (FS)
                                  Mussel Picker (EA) (WP)
                                  Mussel-picker (RP)
                                  Oyster Plover (WT)
                                  Oyster-Catcher (WT)
                                  Oyster-picker (WG)
                                  Pied Oyster Catcher (SM)
                                  Piet (FS)
                                  Sea Magpie (LM)
                                  Sea Pie (EA) (JC) (NF) (WH)
                                  (SM) (FS) (GS) (WT)
                                  Sea-pie (DD)
                                  Seapie (RP),
Partridge,
  Grey   *Perdix perdix*   Common Partridge (WT)
                                  Pairtridge (JF)
                                  Pattheridge (WP)
                                  Partridge (SM) (JD) (GS)
                                  Patridge (JC)
                                  Petrege (WG)
                                  Shearleeks (DD)
Peregrine   *Falco peregrinus* Gabbon Hawk (DD)
                                  Game Hawk (JC)
                                  Goose hawk (WG)
                                  Goshawk (SM)
                                  ? Gosshawk (JD)
                                  Hunting Hawk (DD)
                                  Peregrine Falcon (WT)
Petrel, Storm *Hydrobates pelagicus* Mother Carey's Chicken (SM)
                                  Mother Cary's chicken (RP)

Petrel (SM)
Petricock (RH)

Phalarope,		
Grey	*Phalaropus fulicarius*	Grey Phalarope (SM) (WT)
Pheasant	*Phasianus colchicus*	Faysan (WG)
		Fazian (JC)
		Feasan (XG)
		Fesan (WG)
		Phaisan (JF)
		Phaysin (JM)
		Pheasant (JD) (JM) (WT)
Pigeon, Feral	*Columba livia*	Doaffer (JF)
(*see also* Dove, Rock)		Dung-picker (JF)
Pigeon,		
Wood	*Columba palumbus*	Cushat (RH) (TS) (WT)
		Quest (JC)
		Ring Dove (JC) (NF) (WG) (SH) (HM) (SM)
		Ring-Dove (WT)
		Wild Pigeon (JC) (SH) (WG)
		Wilepigeon (JF)
		Wood pigeon (NF)
		Wood-quest (WT)
		Woodpigeon (WT)
		Woodquest (DD) (JM) (JM)
Pintail	*Anas acuta*	Cran Wigeon (CD)
		Lady Duck (RP)
Pipit,		
Meadow	*Anthus pratensis*	Lesser Field Lark (SM)
		Meadow Pipit (WT)
		Moss Cheeper (NF) (XG) (HM) (TM)
		Moss-cheeper (EA) (JC) (NF) (WT)
		Mosscheeper (DD) (JF) (WG) (SH) (WP)

		Moss-creeper (JMy)
		Moss Cheepuck (CS)
		Mossy (JMy)
		Tit Lark (SM)
		Tit-lark (GS)
		Titlark (DD) (WT)
		Tittle (JF)
Pipit, Rock	*Anthus petrosus*	Field-lark (WT)
		Rock-Lark (WT)
		Rock Pipit (WT)
Plover, Golden	*Pluvialis apricaria*	Golden plover (WT)
		? Gray-plover (WH)
		Grey Plover ?(JD) (WG) (SM) (GS) (WT)
		Plover (WG)
		Whistling Plover (JC) (NF)
Plover, Grey	*Pluvialis squatarola*	? Stone Plover (CS)
Plover, Ringed	*Charadrius hiaticula*	Jack Whaup (DD)
		Ringed Dotterel (WT)
		Ringed Plover (SM) (WT)
		Sand Stepper (LM)
		Sand Tripper (EA)
		Sandy-picker (CD)
		Sea Lark (SM)
Pochard	*Aythya farina*	Dun-bird (WT)
		Fresh water wigeon (CS)
		Gold Head (WH) (CS)
		Micawie Duck (HM)
		Pochard (WH) (WT)
		Red-headed Pochard (WT)
		Red Headed Wigeon (CD) (SM)
		Red-headed Widgeon (WH) (WP)

		Red-headed Wigeon (RP)
Puffin	*Fratercula arctica*	Ailsa Cock (RP) (WP) (CS) (WT)
		Ailsa Parrot (CS)
		Bridle-neb (JC)
		Coulter-neb (DD) (WP)
		Coulterneb (WT)
		Dooker (WG)
		Fooran (WP)
		Puffin (SM) (GS) (WT)
		Redneb (FS)
		Sea Parrot (SM) (WT)
Quail	*Coturnix coturnix*	Common Quail (SM) (WT)
		Weep-m'-feet (DD)
		Wet-me-fut (JC)
		Wet-my-foot (SM)
		Wet-my-Foot (NF) (WP)
		Wet-my-Lip (PW)
Rail, Water	*Rallus aquaticus*	Seggan Runner (WG)
		Watter Quail (JF)
		Water Rail (SM)
		Wee Water Hen (JC)
Raven	*Corvus corax*	Corbie (DD) (GD) (RH) (JM) (?TS)
		Raven (SM) (GS) (WT)
Razorbill	*Alca torda*	Couter-Neb (SM)
		Cutty (RP) (WP)
		Diver (LM)
		Puffin (JC) (WG) (XG) (RP) (CS) (WT)
		Razor Bill (SM)
		Razorbill (WT)
		Sea parrot (DD)
		Sea Pigeon (DD)
Redpoll	*Carduelis flammea*	Grey (WP)
		Hedge Grey (WP)

		King Harry (WG)
		Lesser Redpole (WG) (WT)
		Nettley-grey (JF)
		? Red Gray (WS)
		Red linnet (GS)
		Rosy grey (JO)
		Speevy Grey (NF)
		Thorn Grey (JC) (DD) (WP) (WT)
		Thorny-grey (WG)
		Whin Grey (SH) (WP)
Redshank	*Tringa totanus*	Red Shank (SM)
		Red-shank (WH)
		Redshank (WT)
		Ridshank (JF)
Redwing	*Turdus iliacus*	Felt (WP) (WT)
		Redwing (SM) (WT)
		Small felt (WT)
		Wind Thrush (SM)
Robin	*Erithacus rubecula*	Rabbin (RH)
		Red-breast (GD) (GS) (WT)
		Roabin (JF)
		Robin (NF) (TG) (TS) (WT)
		Robin Redbreast (NF) (SM)
		Robin-red-breast (WH)
Rook	*Corvus frugilegus*	Corbie (JF) (RH) (JM) ?(TS)
		Corby (JM)
		Craw (?GD) (WP)
		Crow (JC) (JF) (NF) (HM) (WP)
		Rook (DD) (WG) (XG) (SM) (GS)
Sanderling	*Calidris alba*	Curwillet (SM)
		Sanderling (SM)
Sandpiper, Common	*Actitis hypoleucos*	Common Sandpiper (SM)

		Fresh-water Sandlark (WT)
		Sand Lark (SM)
		Sand Piper (JD)
		Sandlark (HM)
		Summer Snipe (JC)
Scaup	*Aythya marila*	Black Wigeon (CD) (RP)
		Scaup Duck (SM)
Scoter,		
Common	*Melanitta nigra*	Black diver (GS)
		Black duck (CD) (RP) (WT)
		Black Scoter (WT)
		Black Wigeon (WG)
		Common Scoter (WT)
Shag	*Phalacrocorax*	
	aristotelis	Crested Cormorant (RP)
		Crested Corvorant (SM)
		Diver (CD)
		Green cormorant (RP)
		Green Diver (WG)
		Scart (RP)
		Shag (SM)
		Shagge (WH)
		Sheg (JF)
		Skarf (JC)
		Skart (EA) (JC)
Shearwater,		
Manx	*Puffinus puffinus*	Herring Hawk (FS)
		Mackerel-cock (CD) (RP)(WP) (WT)
		Manx Puffin (WP)
		Manx Shearwater (WT)
Shelduck	*Tadorna tadorna*	Ber-gander (WH)
		Burrough Duck (WP)
		Burrough-duck (WH)
		Burrow duck (CD) (RP) (WT)
		Scale-drake (SH) (WP)

		Scaledrake (SH) (FS)
		Shel-drake (WH)
		Sheld duck (EA)
		Shelldrake (RP) (WT)
		Sheldrake (JD) (GS)
		Shellduck (WG)
		Shiel Drake (SM)
		Shieldrake (WG) (WT)
		Skeelduck (XG)
		Skeldrake (WH)
Shoveler	*Anas clypeata*	Shoveller (SM)
		Spoonbill (CD)
		Spoonbill Duck (NF)
		White-sided Diver (JC)
Siskin	*Carduelis spinus*	Aberdevine (JF) (WT)
		Siskin (WT)
Skua, Arctic	*Stercorarius parasiticus*	Black-toed Gull (SM)
		Dirt Bird (SM) (WP)
		Dirtbird (FS)
		Dung Bird (SM)
		Dung-hunter Gull (GS)
		Kepshite (FS)
		Richardson's Skua (WT)
		Shite (DD)
		Snapshite (DD)
Skua, Great	*Stercorarius skua*	Allan Hawk (WH) (RP) (WP)
		Gab-shite (WG)
		Gannet (WH)
		Great Grey Gull (SM)
		Grey Gull (SM)
		Skua (WH) (SM) (WT)
Skylark	*Alauda arvensis*	Common Lark (WT)
		Field Lark (SM)
		Lark (TG) (HM) (SM)
		Laverock (DD) (GD) (RH)
		(WG) (JM) (SM) (ST)

		Lavrock (TS)
		Leverock (JF)
		Sky Lark (SM)
		Sky-lark (GS)
		Skylark (WT)
Snipe	*Gallinago gallinago*	Common Snipe (WT)
		Guttersnipe (DD)
		Heather Bleat (DD) (WG) (WP)
		Heather-bleat (HM)
		Heather bleater (SM) (CS) (WT)
		Heatherbleat (JF)
		Snipe (JD) (SM) (GS)
Snipe, Jack	*Lymnocriptes minimus*	Jack Snipe (JD) (SM) (WT)
		Jack-snipe (GS)
		Weather blate (GS)
Sparrow, House	*Passer domesticus*	House Sparrow (GS) (SM) (WT)
		Spadger (JO)
		Sparrow (TG)
		Tree Sparrow (SH)
Sparrow, Hedge		*see* Dunnock
Sparrow, Tree	*Passer montanus*	Mountain Sparrow (WT)
		Tree Sparrow (WT)
		White cap (GS)
Sparrowhawk	*Accipiter nisus*	Blue hawk (SH)
		Finlay's Hawk (DD)
		Hawk (JC)
		Kak (WG)
		Sparrow Hawk (GS)
		Sparrow-hawk (SM) (WT)
Starling	*Turnus vulgaris*	Common Stare (SM)
		Dirtbird (DD)
		Snowburd (JF)

		Stair (EA)
		Star (JC) (JF) (NF) (HM) (TM)
		Stare (DD) (WG) (SM) (WT)
		Starlin' (TG)
		Starling (SM) (GS) (WT)
Stonechat	*Saxicola rubicola*	Black-cap (WT)
		Blackcap (WG) (CD)
		Moor Titling (SM)
		Stanechakker (JF)
		Stone Checker (GM) (TM)
		Stonechacker (DD)
		Stone-chat (SM) (WT)
		Stone-chatter (SM) (GS)
		Stone-checker (NF) (♂WP)
		Stonechecker (SH)
		Whin Checker (JC)
		? Whin-chat (TS)
		Whin-checker (CD) (NF) (♀WP)
		Whinchat (CD)
Swallow	*Hirundo rustica*	Chitterling (WP)
		Common Swallow (SM) (WT)
		Swalla (JF)
		Swallow (TG) (GS)
Swan, Mute	*Cygnus olor*	Tame Swan (JD) (WH) (RP)
Swan, Whooper	*Cygnus cygnus*	Elk (WH) (WP)
		Great Wild Swan (WT)
		Hooper (WH) (WT)
		Swan (JD) (GS)
		Whistling Swan (WT)
		Wild Swan (WH) (SM) (RP)
Swift	*Apus apus*	Black Martin (SM) (CD)
		Common Swift (WT)
		Swallow (HM)
		Swift (SM) (GS)

Teal	*Anas crecca*	Teal (JD) (SM) (GS) (WT)
		Teal Duck (HM)
Tern, Arctic	*Sterna paradisaea*	Arctic Tern (WT)
		Sea Swallow (JC) (CS)
Tern, Common	*Sterna hirundo*	Great Tern (SM)
		Pirre (CS) (WT)
		Sea Swallow (JC) (SM) (WT)
		Spurre (CS)
Thrush, Mistle	*Turdus viscivorus*	Cornageerie (HM)
		Corney-garey (DD)
		Corney Keevor (CS)
		Corny-gera (WP)
		Corny-keevor (WP) (WT)
		Grey felt (JF)
		Felt (JF) (WG) (SH)
		Felt Thrush (JC)
		Jay (JF) (NF) (TM) (WP) (CS) (WT)
		Jay Thrush (JC) (NF)
		Missel Thrush (SM) (WT)
		Misseltoe Thrush (SM)
		Mistletoe Thrush (JC)
		Screech Cock (NF) (JC) (WP)
		Screech Thrush (JO)
		Screech-cock (JD)
		Screech-thrush (JF)
		Skirley (WG)
		Snaburd (JF)
		Snaeburd (JF)
		Snawcock (CD)
		Snowburd (JF)
		Snowcock (HM)
		Storm Cock (JC)
Thrush, Song	*Turdus philomelos*	Common Thrush (WT)

		Mavis (DD) (JF) (TG) (EA) (TS)
		Mavish (GD) (WK)
		Song Thrush (SM) (WT)
		Throstle (WG)
		Thrush (HM) (SM) (GS)
Tit, Blue	*Cyanistes caeruleus*	Billy Nipper (TM)
		Billy-biter (WG)
		Blue Bonnet (WG) (SH) (SM) (TM)
		Blue Tit (WT)
		Blue Tit Mouse (SM)
		Blue tit-mouse (GS)
		Blue titmouse (NF) (WT)
		Bluebonnet (DD) (TG) (WP) (WT)
		Tittie-mouse (DD)
		Tittymouse (NF)
		Titty Mouse
		Tomtit (NF) (WT)
		Wee Bluebonnet (JC)
Tit, Coal	*Periparus ater*	Coal Tit (WT)
		Wee blakheid (JF)
Tit, Great	*Parus major*	Big Bluebonnet (JC)
		Black-skull (DD)
		Blakheid (JF)
		Great Blue Bonnet (WP)
		Great blue Tit Mouse (SM)
		Great Tit (WT)
		Kue-Te-Kue (DD)
		Large Blue Titmouse (SM)
		Tom-tit (GS)
Tit, Long-tailed	*Aegithalos caudatus*	Long-tailed Tit (WT)
		Long-tailed tit-mouse (GS)
Titlark	*see* Meadow Pipit	

Treecreeper	*Certhia familiaris*	Woodpecker (JC) (CD) (WG) (SH) (TM)
Tufted duck	*Aythya fuligula*	Tufted Duck (SM)
		White Side (WP)
		White-sided Diver (CD) (NF)
Twite	*Carduelis flavirostris*	Heatherling (WP)
		Heather Grey (JC) (WP) (WT)
		Mountain Grey (JC)
		Mountain linnet (WT)
		Twite (GS)
		Whin-gray (GS)
Wagtail, Grey	*Motacilla cinerea*	Grey Wagtail (SM) (WT)
		Yellow Wagtail (JC) (SH) (SM) (WT)
		? Yellow Water-wagtail (GS)
		Water Wagtail (WP)
		Willy Wagtail (TM)
Wagtail, Pied	*Motacilla alba*	Common wagtail (WT)
		Cow Bird (WG)
		Pied Wagtail (SM) (WT)
		Water Wagtail (GS)
		Wee Willie Wagtail (GM)
		White Wag Tail (SM)
		Willie-wagtail (PW)
		Willy Wagtail (WG) (TM) (NF)
		Willie Wagtail (JC) (DD) (XG) (SH)
		Wullie-wagtail (JF) (TS)
Warbler, Grasshopper	*Locustella naevia*	Grasshopper Warbler (SM) (WT)
		Torie Bird (DD)
Warbler, Sedge	*Acrocephalus schoenobaenus*	Nightingale (NF)
		Sedge bird (SM)

		Sedge Warbler (WT)
		Wee Nightingale (JC)
Warbler,		
Willow	*Phylloscopus trochilus*	Hay-bird (WP)
		Sally Wran (JF) (WG) (WP) (SM) (TM)
		Sally Wren (NF) (DD) (JC)
		? Warbler (TG)
		White Wren (HM)
		Willow Wren (EA) (NF) (WG) (SM)
Wheatear	*Oenanthe oenanthe*	Stanechacker (CS)
		Stone checker (JC) (WT)
		Stone-checker (WP)
		Stonechat (CD)
		Stonechecker (WG) (SH)
		White Rump (SM)
Whimbrel	*Numenius phaeopus*	Jack Courliew (WG)
		Jack Curlew (CD)
		Little Curlew (SM)
		May Bird (EA)
		May Curlew (EA) (LM)
		May Jack (WP)
		May Whaup (CS) (FS)
		Sandlark (DD)
		Whimbrel (SM)
Whinchat	*Saxicola rubetra*	Whinchacker (DD)
		? Whin-chat (TS)
		? Whinchat (SM)
		Whin checker (GM)
		Whinny Grey (WG)
Whitethroat	*Sylvia communis*	Hammer-head (NF)
		Lady Linte White (JC)
		Maggie-Muffie (DD)
		Nettle-grey (SH)
		Nettle-singer (WG)

		White Throat (SM)
		White-throat (WT)
Wigeon	*Anas Penelope*	King Wigeon (JC)
		Whim (SM)
		Widgeon (SM)
		Wigeon (JD) (GS) (WT)
		Wudgeon (JF)
Woodcock	*Scolopax rusticola*	Wood-cock (GS)
		Woodcock (JD) (SM) (WT)
Woodlark	*Lullula arborea*	Wood Lark (SM)
Woodpigeon	*see* Pigeon, Wood	
Wren	*Troglodytes troglodytes*	Chitter Chitty Wren (NF)
		Chitty Wran (TM)
		Chitty-wran (JF)
		Chitty Wren (DD) (WT)
		Chitty-wren (JC) (JM)
		Common Wren (SM) (WT)
		Jenny Wran (WG)
		Jenny wren (WT)
		Jenny Wren (NF) (XG)
		Jinnywran (JM)
		Jinny-wran (JF)
		Tit (WG)
		Titty-wran (WG)
		Tittywran (SH)
		Wran (JF)
		Wren (TG) (GS) (TS)
Yellow-hammer	*Emberiza citrinella.*	Chitterareery (JM)
		Yella Yilder (*per PSR*)
		Yella Yoit (GM)
		Yella-yert (WP)
		Yellayoit(JF) (WP)
		Yellayorlin (JF)
		Yellayornin (JF)
		Yellayowt (JF)

Yellow Ammer (WT)
Yellow Bunting (NF) (WT)
Yellow Hammer (NF) (GM)
(SM) (GS)
Yellow Yearling (WG)
Yellow Yeldren (SH)
Yellow Yelldren (WG)
Yellow Yerling (JC)
Yellow Yoit (DD)
Yellow Yoldrin (XG)
Yellow Yowling (CS)
Yellow Yorl (TM)
Yellow Yorlan (NF)
Yellow Yorlin (NF) (JM) (WT)
Yellow Yorling (TG) (GM)
(SM)
Yellow Yorning (DD)
Yellow Yotie (HW)
Yellow yowley (CS)
Yeltie (NF) (JC) (WG) (NF)
Yilleyyorlin (WP)
Yirlin (WP)
Yoit (TG)
Yolling (CS)

Sources

Listed by the second letter which represents the surname or pseudonym of the compiler.

(**EA**)   Edward Armstrong, *Birds of the grey wind.* 2nd ed. London: Lindsay Drummond, 1944.

(**FB**)   Francis Boyle, poet.

(**JC**)   J. C., 'Hillsborough', *Northern Whig*, 30 November 1907

(**CD**)   C. Douglas Deane, *Handbook of the birds of Northern Ireland.* (1954). Reprint / new ed., Belfast Museum and Art Gallery, [c.1974].

(**DD**)   Dixon Donaldson, 'Islandmagee', *Northern Whig*, 30 November 1907.

(**GD**)   George Dugall, The *Northern Cottage and other poems.* Londonderry: McCorkell. 1824 (glossary).

(**JD**)   John Dubourdieu, *Statistical survey of the County of Antrim.* Dublin: Dublin Society, 1812.

(**JF**)   James Fenton *The hamely tongue.* 2nd ed. Belfast: Ullans Press, 2000.

(**NF**)   N. H. F., 'Hillsborough, Down, Antrim and Tyrone', *Northern Whig*, 30 November 1907; 'North of Ireland, Lough Neagh, South-east Tyrone, County Down', *Northern Whig*, 9 September 1922.

(**TG**)   Thomas Given, *Poems from college and country.* Belfast: Baird, 1900.

(**WG**)   W. H. Given, 'Coleraine', *Northern Whig*, 30 November 1907

(**XG**)   'Gulliver', 'Castlerock', *Northern Whig*, 26 October 1907

(DH) David Herbison, poet.

(RH) Robert Huddleston, poet.

(SH) Sam Henry, 'Coleraine and north Ulster', *Northern Whig*, 30 November 1907.

(WH) Walter Harris, *The antient and present state of the County of Down*. Dublin: Exshaw, 1744.

(SK) Samuel Keightley, novelist

(WK) William J. Knowles ('F. L.'), [nine local glossaries], *Ballymena Observer*, April-August1992 (Academy, merged compilation).

(GM) G. L. Moore, 'General gloss[a]ry of local words, Bangor, Co. Down', ms. 1942.

(HM) H. G. McW, 'Monlough, Co. Down', *Northern Whig*, 21 July 1923.

(JM) John J. Marshall, 'The dialect of Ulster: glossary of words in the Ulster dialect, chiefly used in the midland and north-western counties', *Ulster Journal of Archaeology*. New series. Vols. 10-12, 1905-1907. [4 articles]

(JMy) John McAvoy, Greyabbey and Portavogie, Academy website.

(LM) L. McL. (or L. M. L.?), 'Strangford Lough,' *Northern Whig*, 16 September & 28 October 1922.

(SM) Samuel M'Skimin, *History and antiquities of ... Carrickfergus* (1811). New ed. by E. J. McCrum. Belfast: Mullan, 1909.

(TM) T. McC., 'Dunadry', *Northern Whig*, 14 October 1922.

(XM) Montgomery glossary, ms. 1961 (personal communication, single citation)

(*per*) Personal communication.

(**JO**) J. O., 'Belfast', *Northern Whig*, 23 September 1922.

(**RP**) Robert Lloyd Patterson, *Birds, fishes and cetacea commonly frequenting Belfast Lough* London: David Bogue; Belfast Marcus Ward, 1880.

(**WP**) W. H. Patterson, *Glossary of words and phrases used in the counties of Antrim and Down* . London: Trübner for the English Dialect Society, 1880.

(**CS**) Charles Swainson, *Provincial names and folklore of British birds* (London: Trübner for the English Dialect Society, 1885).

(**FS**) F. J. Simms, 'Donaghadee', *Northern Whig*, 26 October 1907.

(**GS**) George Sampson, *Statistical survey of the County of Londonderry*. Dublin: Dublin Society, 1802; and, *A memoir explanatory of the chart and survey of the County of London-Derry, Ireland*. London: Nicol, 1814.

(**TS**) Thomas Stott, 'The Ornithologist', *Belfast Commercial Chronicle*, 1805.

(**ST**) Samuel Thomson, poet.

(**WT**) William Thompson, *Natural history of Ireland. Birds*. 3 vols. London: Reeve, Benham and Reeve, 1849-1851.

Notes

The list passed to me as by W. H. Kiven has been interpreted as by **W. H. Given**.

Barnacle Goose/Brent Goose. Thompson (iii, 46) says of the Bernacle, or White-faced bernacle, *Anser bernicla* (Flem.) and *Anser leucopsis* (Bechst.): "Is a regular winter visitant to the coast". Under the Bernacle, and commenting on Harris's use of the term "land bernacle", Thompson says (iii, 47): "*Land* barnacle is however, a common name for the species now under special consideration, and a distinctive one, as the bird spends much of its time on land, whereas the other barnacle, properly called the brent goose, lives wholly on the water and the sea-banks." Of the Brent Goose, *Anser brenta* (Flem.) and *Anser bernicla* (Linn.), Thompson says: "Is, except in summer, a constant inhabitant of suitable localities around the coast". And (iii, 46), "The brent goose, on the contrary, revels in the soft oozy bays where the *Zostera marina*, or grass-wrack, grows profusely, and on it alone is content to feed."

Bean Goose/Greylag Goose/White-fronted Goose. Thompson says of the Grey Lag Goose, *Anas anser* (Linn.) and *Anser ferus* (Gessner): "is of occasional, but rare occurrence in winter". He says (iii, 29): "The Grey Lag Goose is unknown to my correspondents in the south, and has never come under notice of ornithologists in the north of Ireland." Referring to a specimen of the Grey Lag examined by him in 1837, Thompson says (iii, 28): "This is the first Irish specimen of the true Wild Goose or Grey Lag that I have seen, the Bean Goose being in this country, as in England and Scotland, the common species, and, with the White-fronted, being on sale in our markets every winter." Under the Bean Goose (*Anas/Anser segetum*) Thompson says (iii, 33): "This is *the* wild goose and the bird to whose English name *anser ferus* is often affixed, although this term applies … to the true grey lag".

Harrow Goose. Mentioned by Harris and commented on by Thompson who suggests a wild goose as one of the options. Thompson (iii, 30, 47)

Kite and birds of prey. In discussing the Kite, Thompson (i, 70) says: "The name of 'Kite' appears commonly in the catalogues of birds given in the Statistical Surveys of the Irish counties and elsewhere; but as the larger species of *Falconidae* are in some places called Kite and Glead, as well as Goshawk and Goose-hawk, there can be no doubt that the buzzard, or some common species, was generally meant." Of Buzzards, Thompson (i. 75) remarks: "… The gamekeeper at Tollymore Park states, … that they [buzzards] are known by the names of kite and glead …".

Under **Goshawk** (i, 62), Thompson says: "Cannot be included in the Irish fauna with certainty."

The **Woodlark**, *Lullula arborea*, is identified by M'Skimin but dismissed by Patterson's note as being 'extinct here for many years'.

Thompson (ii, 318) says of the **Spotted Crake,** *Porzana porzana,* that it should be regarded only "with certainty as an occasional – though probably a regular – summer visitant". Wilson and Carmody omit it.

Works consulted

Edward A. Armstrong, *Birds of the grey wind*, 2nd ed. (London: Lindsay Drummond, 1944).

John Braidwood, 'Local bird names in Ulster: a glossary', *Ulster Folklife*, vol. 11, 1965, pp. 98-135. And supplements in vol. 12, 1966, pp. 104-107; vol. 17, 1971, pp. 81-84; vol. 24, 1978, pp. 83-87; vol. 33, 1987, pp. 83-85.

C. Douglas Deane, *Handbook of the birds of Northern Ireland* (1954). Reprint / new ed. Belfast Museum and Art Gallery, [c.1974?].

Clive D. Hutchinson, *Birds in Ireland* (Calton: Poyser for the Irish Wildbird Conservancy, 1989).

Robin Jackson, *A guide to Scots bird names,* Rev. ed. (Banchory: Ptarmigan Press, 2013).

Anthony McGeehan, *Birds: through Irish eyes* (Cork: Collins, 2012).

Robert F. Ruttledge, *Ireland's birds: their distribution and migrations* (London: Witherby, 1966).

Lars Svensson, *Collins bird guide,* 2nd ed. (London: HarperCollins, 2009).

Charles Swainson, *Provincial names and folk lore of British birds* (London: Trübner for the English Dialect Society, 1885).

William Thompson, *The natural history of Ireland. Birds,* Vols 1-3 (London: Reeve, Benham and Reeve, 1849-1851).

Richard J. Ussher and Robert Warren, *The birds of Ireland: an account of the distribution, migrations and habits of birds as observed in Ireland, with all additions to the Irish list* (London: Gurney and Jackson, 1900).

Jim Wilson and Mark Carmody, *The birds of Ireland: a field guide* (Cork: Collins Press, 2013).

Wright, Joseph (ed.). The *English Dialect Dictionary: being the complete vocabulary of all dialect words still in use, or known to have been in use during the last two hundred years.* 6 vols. (Oxford: Frowde, 1898-1905).

www.ingramcontent.com/pod-product-compliance
Lightning Source LLC
Chambersburg PA
CBHW071528040426
42452CB00008B/920